PRACTICAL GUIDE TO

CHILD

PROTECTION

The Challenges, Pitfalls and Practical Solutions

JOANNA NICOLAS

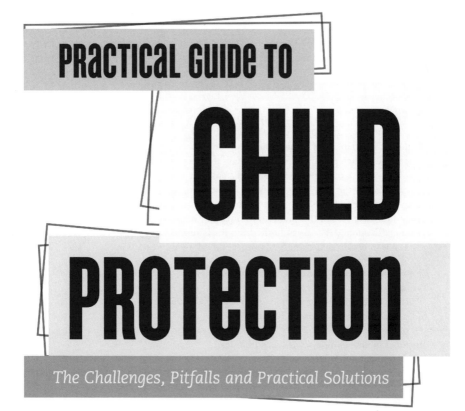

Jessica Kingsley *Publishers*
London and Philadelphia

First published in 2015
by Jessica Kingsley Publishers
73 Collier Street
London N1 9BE, UK
and
400 Market Street, Suite 400
Philadelphia, PA 19106, USA

www.jkp.com

Library of Congress Cataloging in Publication Data
Nicolas, Joanna.
  Practical guide to child protection : the challenges, pitfalls and practical solutions / Joanna Nicolas.
     pages cm
  Includes bibliographical references and index.
  ISBN 978-1-84905-586-4 (alk. paper)
1. Child welfare--Great Britain. 2. Child abuse--Great Britain--Prevention. 3. Social work with children--Great Britain. I. Title.
  HV751.A6N53 2015
  362.70941--dc23
                                        2015005196

British Library Cataloguing in Publication Data
A CIP catalogue record for this book is available from the British Library

ISBN 978 1 84905 586 4
eISBN 978 1 78450 032 0

Printed and bound in Great Britain

PRACTICAL GUIDE TO

CHILD

PROTECTION

of related interest

**The Common-Sense Guide to Improving
the Safeguarding of Children**
Three Steps to Make a Real Difference
Terry McCarthy
ISBN 978 1 84905 621 2
eISBN 978 1 78450 092 4

Eradicating Child Maltreatment
**Evidence-Based Approaches to Prevention
and Intervention Across Services**
Edited by Arnon Bentovim and Jenny Gray
Foreword by Harriet Ward
ISBN 978 1 84905 449 2
eISBN 978 0 85700 823 7

Recognizing and Helping the Neglected Child
Evidence-Based Practice for Assessment and Intervention
*Brigid Daniel, Julie Taylor and Jane Scott with
David Derbyshire and Deanna Neilson*
ISBN 978 1 84905 093 7
eISBN 978 0 85700 274 7

The Child's World
The Comprehensive Guide to Assessing Children in Need
Second Edition
Edited by Jan Horwath
ISBN 978 1 84310 568 8
eISBN 978 0 85700 183 2

The Social Worker's Guide to Children and Families Law
Second Edition
Lynn Davis
ISBN 978 1 84905 440 9
eISBN 978 0 85700 814 5

Direct Work with Vulnerable Children
Playful Activities and Strategies for Communication
Audrey Tait and Helen Wosu
ISBN 978 1 84905 319 8
eISBN 978 0 85700 661 5

The Survival Guide for Newly Qualified Social Workers
Second Edition
Hitting the Ground Running
Helen Donnellan and Gordon Jack
ISBN 978 1 84905 533 8
eISBN 978 0 85700 955 5

Contents

UCB
285936

Introduction

It would be hard to think of many things that are more important than protecting children in our country, and doing all that we can to stop them from being abused or even dying. It sounds so simple, but as those of us that work in this field know, it is hugely challenging and complex work, not just for social workers, but for all the other agencies that play a pivotal role in the work that we all do, trying to ensure that children are safe, protected and thriving. The aim of this book is to help those of you who are working tirelessly to do just that. It is exactly as it says on the cover – 'a practical guide'. There are many excellent academic textbooks informing and supporting practice. There are many books on social work theory, how social work has evolved etc. etc. This is not such a book. The purpose of this book is to help all of you who work in child protection deal with all the practical elements of the work that you do, the issues that you grapple with, every single day. I have also written it for those of you who work with adults – we need housing officers, probation officers, mental health workers, drugs workers, domestic abuse workers, those in the voluntary sector and everyone else who works with adults to be thinking about the child. This book is for you, to help at a time when we all need all the help we can get.

What I want to emphasise is that I am not an academic and this is an individualistic book written by a practitioner with more than 20 years' experience. Throughout the book there is consistent reference to research but much of what is written is my own view of what works and what does not work.

This book is also intended to help the police, teachers, children's centre workers, health visitors and school nurses and all those working with children. Their day-to-day work includes child protection, but their training in this area during qualifying is minimal, if there is any at all. There are also many other professionals who work with adults that I have mentioned who are seeing, or know of, or should be thinking of, children who may be vulnerable whose pre-qualifying training may include nothing about child protection. For all these professionals, unless they work in specialist teams, or specialist roles, their child protection training post-qualifying may be negligible.

This book is here to help to fill that gap. There will be many references to social work and social workers because they are the lead professionals in all child protection cases, but they could not do the work they do effectively without the multi-agency professional network around them and around the child. As the saying goes, 'We are all in this together.' Our best chance of improving a child's life and, in some cases, saving a child's life, will be if we all understand what our roles and responsibilities are, and if we all work closely together. In order to do that, we need to develop a much greater understanding of what good working together looks like, and why we often find it so hard to achieve. This book will help you do that, and it is here to help with challenges you are presented with every single day.

You may be asking, how do we know what the issues are that we grapple with every single day? Much of our learning comes from serious case reviews. It is a requirement of Local Safeguarding Children Boards to undertake a serious case review whenever a child dies or has been seriously harmed, and it is known or suspected that the child has been maltreated. There may also be a cause for concern as to how agencies have worked together. Serious case reviews are a rich source of learning. Since 2010, 393 serious case reviews have been undertaken. Up until 2011 all of them followed the same methodology. The data was brought together, analysed, and findings were published every two years by M. Brandon and colleagues. In recent years this important source of learning has been lost because Local Safeguarding Children Boards have been able to employ different methodologies when undertaking serious case reviews. This makes it more difficult for researchers to bring the data together to analyse it, although the coalition government did announce, just before the election, that they were going to reintroduce the biannual reviews, which is excellent news.

The children's charity, the NSPCC now holds the national repository of published serious case reviews and also produces thematic analysis of case reviews, which are useful resources in themselves, but they do not replace the comprehensive overview of all serious case reviews produced by Brandon *et al.* This is why, when I make reference to all serious case reviews, the data only goes up until 2011.

It is from those serious case reviews, and from the preceding and subsequent serious case reviews, that we see the areas of work we find the most challenging, and therefore the areas that we need the most assistance with.

There are five areas of practice that come up again and again, and so therefore, by definition, these must be the areas we find the most challenging. They are:

› understanding the impact of neglect and working with neglect cases

› communicating with children and keeping the child at the centre of what we do

› working with families where there is either non-compliance, or disguised compliance

› the impact of multiple risk factors

› communication and information sharing between professionals.

It is for this reason that the first four chapters of this book consider the first four of those points in turn. Communication and information sharing between professionals is considered in Chapter 7.

Seeing and assessing children in their own environment is an essential part of child protection work. Chapter 5 looks at home visiting, and how we can make the most of those visits, and how we do them when a family is openly hostile or aggressive, being clear about what we need to achieve from the visit.

Chapter 6 then examines other areas that we know are challenging for professionals, for example, working with children who are at risk of, or are being, sexually exploited, and working in the child protection arena with children with disabilities or children from the black and minority ethnic (BME) community.

The final chapter, Chapter 7, considers how we can work with families more constructively within the child protection arena. The starting point for all of us working in child protection should be that, 'The best place for a child to grow up is within their own home.' In the majority of cases that is true; in very few, sadly, it is not. Our best chance of achieving this outcome is if we work openly and honestly with families.

What I sincerely hope is that this book is not seen by any to be a criticism of 'feckless' parents. It is for writers with much greater expertise than I to examine how our society works and how unfair and unbalanced it is. This is not a book about the imbalance between the rich and poor. Nor is it a book about the injustice of the gap between the rich and poor becoming wider in times of austerity. I have no expertise in that area. This is a book for frontline practitioners and the reality of what they are dealing with day after day.

There are so many myths about social work and child protection, and we all have a responsibility to dispel them, so this book is full of myth-busters, some of which you will know, and some you may not, but they are there as a reminder for everyone. If families know the reality of the aim of our work, rather than the tabloid view of child protection, we will have a greater chance of working more effectively with them, to make and sustain the changes that need to happen in order to allow children to be safe and free from abuse.

Chapter 7 also considers how, in view of increasing caseloads and ever-tightening budgets and resources, we can work more effectively to protect children. There is no doubt that the quantity of our work would reduce if the quality improved, however, and there are clear, simple strategies we can put in place to improve the quality of our work and thus reduce the quantity. Because of the volume of work, we rush from one meeting to the next, barely having time to make the telephone calls in the car between meetings; lunch is often eaten in meetings, if at all; and workers send emails at midnight and at weekends. The trouble is that what this can result in is work that is superficial – we only have time to skim the surface. Yes, we may be able to tick a box saying the child has been seen, we may get families to sign written agreements with social care saying they will agree to all sorts of things, but have we really got under the skin? Do we really understand the dynamics of that family and what is going on? Or have we merely scratched the surface?

The more superficially we work, the longer we have to keep the case open because we have not understood what is really going on for this child in this family – and the more times a case is closed and then returns, all of this increases the workload. For all of the effort that professionals put in, change often does not happen, and our work can be ineffective. Chapter 7 looks at how we can change that balance, how we can keep focused on the child and work more effectively with families, gathering evidence that will either show us that the family is able to make and sustain the necessary changes, or that they cannot, so that decisions we make are timely and evidence-based.

Sometimes I am conscious when I am delivering child protection training that we go on about the learning from serious case reviews, when a child has died or suffered serious injuries. There will, of course, be much good practice, which should be celebrated and shared. There is an expectation that Local Safeguarding Children Boards will review cases of good practice too, but these are not published, so are not so widely known about. When we undertake a serious case review, we often find many examples of good practice – the trouble is that it is not the time to talk about it, when there has just been a child death.

Much of the brilliant work that is being done in this field goes below the radar, and it is an injustice that there is usually only interest in the work that we do when there has been the terrible tragedy of a child dying or a child having been abused for many years with professionals seemingly turning a blind eye. Every day in my work I see examples of professionals going way beyond what is in their job description because they are completely dedicated to helping those who are most vulnerable in our society, whether that is the children or the parents/carers. Sadly, there is little public interest in that kind of work.

This book is full of case examples from my own practice, which I hope will bring the book alive. No one ever knows it all, and you, as frontline professionals, will be dealing with difficult situations every day. If one of these case examples rings true to you, I hope it will make you realise that you are not alone. We have all been there, and we really are all in this together.

Finally, I promise you that this book is both jargon- and acronym-free. For this book to live up to its title, it needs to be exactly that, practical. How often do you go to meetings and feel you are drowning in acronyms and jargon that you do not understand, but think you are the only person in the room who does not? How often does someone introduce themselves by saying something like, 'I'm a DNG from ASB', and you think you are the only one who does not understand what any of that means? You will most definitely not be the only one. Some professionals use acronyms and jargon as shorthand, but there are also situations where professionals use them to try to impress. Sometimes I ask someone what a particular acronym they have used stands for, and they do not know. If you are part of a multi-agency group working around a child and their family, you need to know who everyone is and what they are doing, and it is your responsibility to ask. But please do not think you are the only person in the room who does not know what the various acronyms or jargon mean, because you will not be.

Case example: Tudor Rose

Many years ago now, I had a five-year career break while I was having my children. One of the first meetings I attended on my return was a child protection conference. I had just been allocated the case, and was the child's social worker. The mother did not attend the conference and there were no other family members there, but there were about 15 professionals sitting around the table.

When we were talking about what all the concerns were, one of the professionals started listing all the drugs this mother was using, including heroin, methadone, crack and Tudor Rose. Everyone was sitting there looking terribly concerned about all these drugs, but all I could think was that I did not know what Tudor Rose was. I was worried that I would look stupid if I said that because I had spent the last five years immersed in nappies and banana, and Tudor Rose was probably a new drug that was now as well known as methadone, particularly because everyone was shaking their heads about how serious this was. Because I am who I am, I had to ask, and when I did, the worker who had been talking about this looked at me in contempt – she really did – and said witheringly, 'it's sherry'. When she said it, it was quite clear that no one else in that room had the faintest idea what Tudor Rose was, but they had all just been going along with her and no one wanted to ask the question. I have since learnt that Tudor Rose is, to put it politely, very affordable sherry, often seen by park benches.

People often say to me now, 'Can I ask a Tudor Rose question?' It has become a cliché to say 'there is no such thing as a silly question', but a cliché is a cliché because it is true. There really is no such thing as a silly question. Please ask the questions. If we are going to do the best job we can to protect children, we need to keep asking questions, of each other, and of the families we work with.

Language used in this book

Although there has been an increase in the number of fathers who are the primary carers of the children, it is still a small percentage in relation to women. (According to the charity Gingerbread, it is around 8 per cent.[1]) So the majority of primary carers in the UK are women, and this figure is thought to be greater in families where there are child protection concerns – it remains unusual to be working with a family where the father is the primary carer, particularly of young children. For practical reasons, therefore, throughout the book I refer to the mother as the primary carer of the children, but this is not to overlook those fathers who are primary carers.

A parent is defined as meaning a person acting as a father, mother or guardian to a child. This role may be played by a variety

---

1   Gingerbread (no date) 'Statistics.' Available at www.gingerbread.org.uk/content/365/Statistics

of individuals including the child's natural mother or father, a step-parent, a natural parent's partner, a foster or adoptive parent, or a relative or other person acting as a guardian or carer.

1 The Impact of Neglect

Put simply, professionals underestimate the impact of neglect. At the start of this chapter we should remind ourselves what the legal definition of neglect is, but before you read this, test yourself. Cover up the text under 'Remember…', and try to write down what the definition is. This is something I ask professionals to do when I am delivering training about the impact of neglect because professionals always say it is the hardest area of work, the hardest to define, and the hardest to determine at what point and at what level we should intervene. In my experience, many professionals do not actually know what the definition consists of.

REMEMBER…

Neglect is the persistent failure to meet a child's basic physical and/or psychological needs, likely to result in the serious impairment of the child's health or development.

Neglect may occur during pregnancy as a result of maternal substance abuse. Once a child is born, neglect may involve a parent or carer failing to:

> provide adequate food, clothing and shelter (including exclusion from home or abandonment)

> protect a child from physical and emotional harm or danger

> ensure adequate supervision (including the use of inadequate care givers)

> ensure access to appropriate medical care or treatment.

> ›   It may also include neglect of, or unresponsiveness
>   to, a child's basic emotional needs.[1]

Let me ask you two questions: Do you think neglect is as damaging as other types of maltreatment? Do you think our professional response to neglect cases differs to that of other types of maltreatment? If you answered 'yes' to both questions, as most people do, that is where the incongruity lies, but why is that? I hope this chapter will provide some answers.

First of all, let us be clear. Neglect is every bit as damaging as other types of maltreatment, if not more. Children die as a result of neglect, and yet our response in neglect cases often differs to our response to other types of maltreatment. Even the language gives a subconscious message. We talk about 'abuse and neglect' as if neglect is not quite as bad as abuse. Neglect is a form of abuse just as physical, emotional and sexual abuse are also forms of abuse. No one category is worse or less terrible than another, each case is different, and all components have to be taken into consideration.

Assessments should always be made on a case-by-case basis. The reason why many research studies conclude that neglect is more damaging than other types of maltreatment is because we will leave a child in a home when we know there is neglect of that child, but we would not if we knew there was sexual abuse, or ongoing physical abuse, so we can do the research about the long-term impact of neglect because there are so many children who have lived with chronic neglect. We do not have nearly the same numbers of children who have lived with chronic physical or sexual abuse. We know that neglect is the most common form of child abuse. We have more children on a child protection plan as a result of neglect than of any other category of abuse – for many years it has been nearly half of all children on child protection plans. One of the reasons for this is because we underestimate the damage done by neglect. It is also because neglect is all encompassing, and particularly at

---

1   Department for Education (2013) *Working Together to Safeguard Children: A Guide to Interagency Working to Safeguard and Promote the Welfare of Children.* London: Department for Education.

the beginning of the process, when we are starting to look at what is going on in more detail, it is a catch-all category. This is fine at the beginning of the process, but not as time goes on and the child is allowed to remain in the family home, subjected to neglect every single day, without the support being put in place earlier on that may have prevented the situation escalating. And neglect not only affects young children; it also has a huge impact on older children too.

It is very telling that we talk about chronic neglect in present terms, when a child is still living in the home. The only other time we use the word 'chronic' around maltreatment is when we describe historical abuse, usually sexual. If we know a child is being sexually abused, we would not leave them in the home, unprotected – the same is true of physical abuse, but we are much more likely to leave a child who is being neglected in the home, where they live with maltreatment every day of their lives.

REMEMBER...

Neglect cases are often those where professionals will say when talking about the mother, 'but she really loves them.' In cases of maltreatment it is much less common to come across mothers who do not love their children, as opposed to just not being able to put their child's needs first. I have worked with heroin addicts who leave their babies alone while they become sex workers to pay for their drugs. The money then goes on drugs, not food, nappies, warmth and shelter – but those mothers have not hated their babies. They love them, as most mothers do, but their own problems have taken over, their life is consumed by their own needs, and they cannot prioritise their child's needs above their own. So remember, when we look at strengths and concerns in a family, it would always be a concern if we did not think the mother loved her child, but it is not necessarily a strength if she does.

There are many other reasons why neglect is the most common form of child abuse. It is an act of omission, rather than an act of commission. To physically or sexually abuse a child, you have to actually do something. Emotional abuse is either as a result of the child witnessing or hearing the abuse of another, or through deliberate emotional maltreatment of that child. The child is neglected by the parent or carer doing nothing. In the majority of cases where children are being neglected to a level that there are child protection concerns, there will be issues around domestic abuse, adult mental ill health and substance abuse.

The popular press often paints a picture of cold, heartless parents deliberately neglecting their children, but we know that it is more complicated than this. The parents we are working with will very often have real needs of their own. Why have they turned to drugs or alcohol? How did they develop mental ill health? Why have they become a victim or perpetrator of domestic abuse? The correlation between those parents being victims of abuse in their own childhood and perpetrators in adulthood is very high.

Case example: The vulnerability of parents we work with

I was working with a family in which there was domestic abuse, alcohol abuse, emotional abuse and neglect. The mother had five children, the last two by 'Mike'.[2] Mike had a history of violence and alcohol abuse. He had spent a number of years in prison, as a result of his violence that was directed at his partner, the police and anyone who got in his way. His behaviour was notorious, and there were many local press reports about him. Prior to arrest, or when in a fight, he would bite into a glass bottle to cut his mouth, and would then spit blood, saliva and glass at his opponent, or the police. He would also bite police officers, if given a chance, and whenever the police were called to an incident that they knew involved Mike, a minimum of six officers would attend. It was said that Mike hated anyone in a position of authority. As a perpetrator of domestic

---

2   All names and other identifying features throughout the book have been changed.

abuse, his partner would often have a bruised eye; she once had a broken arm from him twisting it, as well as frequent cigarette burns. (I am only telling you about some of his offences because many of his others were so uniquely macabre and sick that they may lead to identification.)

Mike flitted in and out of the family, and when he was there he could cause havoc and fear. We were working with the mother, helping and supporting her to leave Mike, which is what she said she wanted to do, but because of all the complexities of domestic abuse, we were not sure she would be able to leave him. We had to ensure the children were safe.

It was agreed early on that because of the nature of the concerns we would go to court to seek interim care orders[3] in respect of the children, and recommend to the court that all contact with Mike stopped while we assessed the situation and considered whether continued contact would be in the best interests of the children, and if that was the case, how that could be managed safely. It was my job to tell Mike what we were proposing.

I had never met Mike before; he was an elusive character and apparently felt about social workers as he did about the police. In arranging the meeting, consideration had to be given to my personal safety. We knew that when he got angry he would throw whatever he could pick up at people, so we arranged the meeting in a room with two exits, so he could not prevent us leaving through one, and we took everything out of the room, except for three chairs – I was accompanied by another social worker. We also had two police officers hiding in a room just outside one exit, and another two hiding by the other exit. Mike hated the police, and we knew that if he saw them, he was likely to explode.

All this took a while to set up, and this, combined with the press and police reports I had read about Mike, meant that by the time I was told he was there, the adrenaline was pumping and my heart was racing. I walked to reception expecting to be met by a six-foot hulk, spitting and swearing and threatening. Instead, there was one figure sitting in reception. He was small and shrunken, and looked

---

3   Interim care orders are temporary orders granted by the court, and give the local authority shared parental responsibility with the parents. They permit a temporary arrangement for care of a child to be imposed for up to eight weeks in the first instance.

very frightened. In that moment it hit me how the perpetrators we work with are victims of life themselves.

Throughout our meeting Mike sat quietly. He cried quietly and accepted everything I said. He kept apologising.

Mike was unable to read and write and had a very limited vocabulary and had grown up with a vicious father and a mother who drank to blot out the fear in her life. Mike could not remember how long he had lasted at school, but it was not very long. He had learnt from his parents that how you operate in life is to hit people and drink, and that is what he did and it was all he knew. He had never worked; he went from woman to woman, and did not know how many children he had; but what had Mike's life chances ever been?

None of that excuses the terrible things Mike did, but they do explain them.

In neglect cases, most of the parents we are working with are not deliberately harming their children, and it is this that can affect how we respond. Most of us would feel very differently about a cold, calculating sex offender to a couple who were neglecting their children because of their own life experiences.

Domestic abuse and neglect

The links between domestic abuse and child abuse are irrefutable, not only in terms of the emotional impact on the child of witnessing or hearing domestic abuse, but also the risks of physical abuse either directed at the child or caused when the child tries to protect the victim, and also in terms of neglect.

Perpetrators of domestic abuse can be male or female, as can victims, but in the UK the majority of perpetrators are male and the majority of victims are female. The mother who is a victim of domestic abuse may very well turn to alcohol, or other substances, as a coping mechanism, and may very well develop mental ill health as a result of the abuse.

We look at these multiple risk factors in greater detail in Chapter 4, so for now all we need to think about is that, for very understandable reasons, there are very strong links between these three risk factors, between domestic abuse, substance misuse and mental ill health.

Myth: 'Why doesn't she just leave him?'

It seems so simple. Most of us would say that if our partner laid a finger on us, he would be gone, or we would be gone, but of course it is not that simple, otherwise victims of domestic abuse would just leave. There are many reasons why it is so hard, apart from the psychological process (see below). Even the mothers who are financially independent and have somewhere to go, and there are not many of those, struggle to leave. There may be threats of killing the children, the pets, themselves. He says he will tell everyone what the mother is like, what a terrible mother she is, social services will take the children away, and so it goes on.

The mother knows she will lose her home, she has nowhere to go, the children will leave all their friends and so, ironically, she decides to stay for the sake of the children. So many mothers have said to me over the years, 'It's not that bad. I can put up with the odd beating, but we keep our home, and I don't want to disrupt the kids.'

The way the perpetrator grooms a victim of domestic abuse is similar to how a paedophile grooms a child. It is a complex psychological process, where the victim is drawn in over time. The perpetrator is not going to punch the woman on the first date. Perpetrators often choose their victims carefully – the girl or woman who does not value herself, who thinks she is worth no more (although I have met perpetrators who say they like the challenge of a 'strong' woman). The control is often very subtle, and when the balance tips from caring and protective to controlling and abusive, the victim is usually told it is her fault, and because she is told it enough times, she believes it.

Case example: The power of domestic abuse

Almost from the point they were married, Sue's partner started to be violent towards her. She was not allowed to see her friends and family. She was not allowed to work. When she went to the shops, her partner would time her, and if she was late back, he would beat her.

For 15 years he would beat her if she did not put the ketchup bottle on the table, in exactly the right position, and the bottle had to have exactly the right amount of ketchup in it. Tea had to be ready at exactly six o'clock, and if it wasn't, he would beat her; this was regardless of the children's needs, if they had been ill, or if the cooker was not working. In 15 years Sue only told one person once about what life was like at home. She told her mother. Her mother's response was that she should be a better wife and then he would not beat her, which is exactly what her partner said. So for Sue, it was just greater confirmation that it was her fault.

It was not until he started hitting the children that Sue felt she had to speak out. After months of support, she still believes she deserves the way he treats her because that is what she has been told every single day for the last 15 years. She minimises the impact on the children because she is unable to leave him. She said to me recently, 'I know it isn't about the ketchup bottle. If it wasn't that it would be something else', but she cannot leave.

We are getting better at recognising emotional abuse because of the increasing amount of research highlighting the impact on the baby's brain, both in utero and after birth, of witnessing or hearing the abuse of another, that is, domestic abuse. It is an increasingly accepted view that perpetrators of domestic abuse are also perpetrators of child abuse, but it is not yet universally accepted, despite domestic abuse being a factor in 63 per cent of the 139 serious case reviews that took place between 2009–11 in England and Wales, 54 per cent of 56 reviews in Scotland since 2007, and 58 per cent of 24 reviews in Northern Ireland between 2003–08.

What challenges us as professionals is that the mother who is a victim of domestic abuse may very well be doing the best she can to protect her child, but the stark fact is that if she cannot protect herself, she cannot protect her child.

Case example: Protecting the child

I started visiting a mother who had an 18-month-old boy. The health visitor had referred the little boy because his development seemed to be delayed. He was not yet moving around, even on his bottom, and there seemed to be no organic reason for this. The health visitor was also concerned about the mother, who was very anxious about the health visitor visiting the home, and equally reluctant to visit the clinic. Whenever the health visitor asked about her partner, she seemed very frightened, and said he was far too busy to go to any health appointments. When the health visitor first mentioned social care,[4] the mother became very fearful and said her partner would be really angry.

We arranged that I would telephone the mother when we knew the father would not be around, and I arranged the visit similarly. On the day of my first visit it was a beautiful sunny day. I was at the home for an hour-and-a-half, and during that time the mother did not take the little boy out of his pushchair once. He was strapped in, in front of the television, with the curtains half drawn.

What transpired was that when the little boy had started to become mobile, the father would get very angry because the little boy was grabbing things, including the television remote control and the father's cigarettes. The father had made it very clear to the mother that if she did not keep their child under control, he would get hit too. Her only way to do this was to strap him in the pushchair all day. That was why his development was delayed.

In the case example above, the mother was protecting her child in the best way she knew, and while she was protecting him from getting hit, the child's many other needs were being neglected. We see this frequently where domestic abuse is involved.

It can feel as if we are penalising the mother, who is already being told by her partner that she is useless, and now professionals come along and say that on top of that, she cannot look after her children and social workers are going to get involved, and that we are probably going to take her children away from her because she is so useless. (Of course that is not how social workers are putting

---

4   Although most professionals now refer to children's social care, more widely it is still known as social services. It is the same thing.

it, but that is how what they, and other professionals, are saying will be heard.)

Myth: 'Child protection plans help social workers remove children'

One of the greatest myths about the child protection system is that child protection plans are a means for social workers to remove children from their parents. First of all, social workers do not have the power to remove children (this is another myth). Second, that is not what child protection plans are. If we were that concerned, we would go to court to request the child be removed from the family. A child protection plan is put in place if the professionals consider that a child is suffering, or is likely to suffer, significant harm, as defined in the Children Act 1989.[5] What it is actually saying is, 'Yes, we are very concerned about your child, but we hope and believe that with the right amount of support you will be able to make the changes we believe are necessary, in order for your child to be safe and to thrive.'

So why else are the links between domestic abuse and neglect so strong? Because the mother who is a victim of domestic abuse may be unable to put her children's needs before her own, because her way of dealing with the abuse is to drink, or her mental health becomes so severely affected she cannot care for her children, or she has to put her partner first and is told the children need less, and as in the case example above, her way of keeping the child safe may not be enough.

---

5   Harm is defined as the 'ill treatment or the impairment of health or development.' As defined in HM Government (2015) Working Together to Safeguard Children, available at www.gov.uk/government/uploads/system/uploads/attachment_data/file/419595/Working_Together_to_Safeguard_Children.pdf. As a result of the Adoption and Children Act 2002, the definition of harm also includes 'impairment suffered by hearing or seeing the ill-treatment of another.'

Parental substance misuse and neglect

Why is there such a strong link between parental substance misuse and neglect? If parents are misusing a substance, whether it is drugs or alcohol, it will have a significant impact on their ability to care for their child and to prioritise their child's needs. We also know from serious case reviews that when a baby has died as a result of overlay, which is the accidental death by smothering caused by a larger individual sleeping on top of an infant, there are very often drugs or alcohol involved.

According to research by the court welfare service, the Child and Family Court Advisory and Support Service (Cafcass), two thirds of children coming into care do so because the parents are misusing substances, and in the majority of cases the substance misuse will have led to neglect of the child,[6] and that is why the child is removed from the parents.

Because of the illegality and social stigma around using street drugs and a fear of having their children removed, parents are often secretive about their usage. While alcohol may be more socially accepted, we must always be mindful that users of either will usually minimise their usage.

Myth: 'Alcohol makes you violent'

No it does not.[7] Our bodies do not have a physical reaction to alcohol in the sense that it makes us violent. There is no alcohol in this world that makes us become violent. What alcohol does is it reduces our ability to think straight, and it acts as a disinhibitor. There are thousands of people who get drunk regularly, but they do not all go round punching people. Do you want to punch someone when you have too much to drink? Probably not.

---

6   Cafcass (2012) *Three Weeks in November…Three Years On, Cafcass Care Application Study 2012*. London: Cafcass. Available at www.cafcass.gov.uk/media/6437/Cafcass%20Care%20Application%20Study%202012%20FINAL.pdf

7   International Center for Alcohol Policies (ICAP) (no date) 7. Drinking and Violence. Available at www.icap.org/PolicyTools/ICAPBlueBook/BlueBookModules/7DrinkingandViolence/tabid/168/Default.aspx

> The reaction I have to alcohol is that I just want to eat because I think, 'oh sod it'. My inhibitions are gone.
>
> In this country we have a culture of alcohol equals violence. We see it with domestic abuse, with football matches, and in town centres on Friday and Saturday night. It is the culture that links the two, and we know that there is a very strong link between the two, but not a physical reaction. There are religions where alcohol is banned, and there is just as much domestic abuse and violence; it may just manifest itself in different ways.

When a parent is addicted to an illegal drug, their number one priority will be getting that drug, and not only do they have to get that drug, but they also have to pay for it. It is important to remember what I said earlier, and that we saw in the case example of Mike. We know that many people who misuse drugs do so because they are using it as a coping mechanism to deal with maltreatment, including neglect they themselves suffered as children. Although our priority always has to be the protection of the child, this is not to say that we should not feel compassion for the parents too. Coping in a drug-free world is terrifying and unimaginable for many of the parents we work with, and that is usually what we are asking the parent(s) to do.

Mental ill health and neglect

Again, there are very strong links between mental ill health and neglect, but just as alcohol does not equal violence, the mental ill health of a parent does not equal neglect.[8] It depends entirely on whether the parent is willing and/or able to accept they have a mental illness, and whether they are willing to have it treated.

---

8   NSPCC (2013) Neglect and Serious Case Reviews. Available at www.nspcc. org.uk/globalassets/documents/research-reports/neglect-serious-case-reviews-report.pdf

Case example: Working with a parent who has a good understanding of her mental illness

I worked with a mother who had a diagnosis of bipolar disorder. She had a very good understanding of her illness; she took her medication, and worked closely with her community psychiatric nurse and prescribing psychiatrist. By mutual agreement she had shared care of her older children with their father, with whom she no longer lived. The father also looked after the children when she was very unwell and had to be admitted to a psychiatric unit. The only reason social care became involved was because she became pregnant by someone in her block of flats who was very controlling of her. She was frightened of him and wanted to get away. He was a heavy cannabis user, and his mental health had deteriorated to such an extent that he refused to leave his flat. She had to do everything for him. Having a baby is a time for greater consideration when someone has a mental illness, particularly around hormone levels and medication, so she was asking for support, and that is what social care, along with partner agencies, was there to do. When I first met her, she told me all about living with bipolar disorder. She said to me, 'You will know when I am going downhill because I will stop wearing make-up and I will smell.' She wore a lot of make-up and was always very clean.

Social care was there to support her through a tricky time. The agencies all worked really closely together, including housing that moved her, and six months after the baby was born, we closed the case. There were no concerns about the safety or wellbeing of her children, as there had not been before.

There are many parents like this, living with a mental health diagnosis whose children never come to the attention of child protection services because they manage their illness perfectly well, through medication and other means.

It is very sad that there is such a stigma around mental ill health and so people can be reluctant to ask for help. (Someone said to me recently that you do not get sent a 'Get well' card when you are mentally ill. This is so true.) There is a shame attached to something that you may have as little control over chicken pox.

So when I write of mental ill health it is meant in the context of a parent who is unable and/or unwilling to accept their diagnosis and who will not take their medication, or they accept their diagnosis but will not take their medication because they do not like the side effects.

REMEMBER...

You often hear people say, 'She's got mental health.' We all have mental health. Some of us have mental health problems, or mental ill health.

Poverty and neglect

There is, of course, a strong correlation between poverty and neglect. Parents may be exhausted, overwhelmed, stressed, depressed and anxious, with self-esteem destroyed. Some families move from deprivation to destitution, dependent on tenuous voluntary food and clothing banks and with mounting debts. It is not surprising that those families will be likely to struggle to have the energy or composure to parent well despite their best intentions and motivations, but just as mental ill health does not equal neglect, neither does poverty – there are many families living in poverty who care for their children perfectly well, many of whom sacrifice their own needs for the needs of their children. According to Barnardo's, 3.5 million children living in the UK live in poverty, and 1.6 million children live in severe poverty,[9] and the majority of these will not be known to child protection services. There is certainly an argument that more of these children should be offered many more support services, including social care, but in terms of child protection, it is only a small percentage of those children who need child protection services.

---

9   Barnardo's (no date) 'Child poverty statistics and facts.' Available at www. barnardos.org.uk/what_we_do/our_work/child_poverty/child_poverty_ what_is_poverty/child_poverty_statistics_facts.htm

Many of the families that are known to child protection agencies are living in poverty, but this is usually because of how they are spending the very little money that they do have. It is easy to move into the realms of the right-wing newspapers and to talk of flat-screen televisions and Sky TV, but what is unavoidable is the way our society is set up. Parents are expected to prioritise what their children need in terms of food, clothing, shelter, warmth and an environment in which they can thrive. If they are unable or unwilling to do that, for whatever reason, the state has a duty to step in.

I am mindful as I write this that my intention is not to trivialise this subject, nor to underestimate the impact that living in poverty has on families. It is also important to be clear that, as with all of us, there will be an explanation for the way parents behave, and what we as professionals need to do is to look behind the behaviour to try to understand what is causing it – that is what we need to address if changes are going to be made and sustained within a family.

There is no single cause of neglect, but poverty is one of the factors that increases the risk of neglect, along with the other adversities set out above – domestic abuse, mental ill health and substance misuse.

Obesity in childhood

We keep being told there is currently an obesity 'epidemic', and recent figures suggest that 9.3 per cent of all 4- to 5-year-olds are obese, rising to 18.9 per cent of all 17- to 18-year-olds.[10] There is an ongoing debate about whether this should be seen as child abuse. In my view, unless there is a medical reason why the child is obese, if health and education professionals have been trying to work with the parents to help them understand about the impact on the child of being obese, but the parents are unwilling to change and the child continues to put on weight, it should be seen in the context of child protection.

---

10   Health & Social Care Information Centre (2014) *Statistics on Obesity, Physical Activity and Diet: England 2014.* Available at www.hscic.gov.uk/catalogue/PUB13648/Obes-phys-acti-diet-eng-2014-rep.pdf

Case example: The impact of obesity

A head teacher from a primary school came up to me recently and asked me about a child in their school. It is a split-level school. The child has been putting on weight rapidly over the years he has been at school, and is now so overweight that he cannot physically climb the stairs to get to the classrooms upstairs. The head teacher said they had all been trying to work with the parents, but to no avail. Her question was, 'Is that child protection?'

As the definition of neglect starts off, 'Neglect is the persistent failure to meet a child's basic physical and/or psychological needs, likely to result in the serious impairment of the child's health or development', why would it not be?

We are all very clear that if children are malnourished because the parents are starving them, then that would be seen as child protection; the trouble is that there is a terrible anxiety about discussing weight, if the issue is being over- rather than under-weight.

Case example: Discussing obesity – the challenge for professionals

I was the social worker for two siblings under three who had been removed from their parents' care. They were never going to return home, and we needed to find the best place for them to live for the rest of their lives. As we always do, we looked to family first. We were told about an uncle and his wife, who had not been able to have their own children and who really wanted the children to go and live with them. What they were suggesting was that the wife would give up her job and be the primary carer, and the uncle would carry on working. I spoke on the telephone with them, did all the checks, and everything seemed very positive, but then I went to meet them and my heart sank. The wife must have weighed 20 stone. My heart sank for two reasons: first of all, how could she run around after two children under three when she was puffing from answering the door, and also because I was going to have to bring it up.

Much as I wanted to brush it under the carpet and pretend that I hadn't noticed that she had to lever herself up out of a chair, I could not do that. I had to bring it up.

It turned out that she had recently had a gastric band fitted and had lost three stone already and seemed to be going in the right direction. The end result was that it was felt that the benefits for these children of being placed with loving family members, being able to see their mother, who was not considered a risk, and the fact that she was addressing the problem outweighed the considerable concerns about her weight.

The point is, that because many of us find it very awkward to talk about it and are worried about being insensitive, we ignore it, or we justify it by saying the family is terribly poor. An argument is often put forward that it is because of poverty, and yes, there are strong links between poverty and obesity, in adults and in children, but just as with everything else, poverty does not equal obesity, and it is outrageous to suggest that just because someone is poor their children are going to be obese and neglected.

What we need, as with everything else, is for the professionals working with families early on to pick up on a child putting on weight beyond the norm, and to address it then. We need health visitors, doctors, children's centre workers, nursery workers and primary schools to be dealing with it, not turning a blind eye because it is very difficult to talk about it, and then the next thing that happens is a call to social care when the child is so overweight he cannot climb the stairs. If you have been doing this, and it has made no difference and the parents are not listening, or do not seem to care, that is when you need to start thinking about this in the context of child protection. Is the child likely to suffer significant harm as a result of the neglect?

We know about the physical impact on the body of being obese. We know the emotional impact, so why do we not act? We know the prejudice obese people are subjected to, the cruelty, so why do we not act to protect these children before they start down the path of a life that most morbidly obese people describe as abuse, misery and torment?

Both children and adults who are morbidly obese describe how members of the public respond to them when they are out and about. They describe how people stare and pull disgusted faces and laugh.

Some people make derogatory remarks and are aggressive with them. Imagine being faced with that every day. That is the disservice we do to children if we do not step in early on to tackle weight issues.

We also need a consistent approach to obesity in children – it is very unfair to families that in one area your child might be made the subject of a child protection plan, whereas in another no one seems to care.

Neglect is a judgement

The cases that tend to give us the greatest conundrums and that remain with social care the longest are neglect cases, because we are making judgements based on what is 'good enough'.

What is 'good enough' parenting? How clean does your house have to be? Does it matter if the house is a tip but the mother is always playing with her child? Sometimes the mother is very low but then she picks up again. Sometimes the home is in a state, but other times it is better. What happens with many neglect cases is that things may be very worrying but then they get a bit better and then worse and then better again – at what point do we intervene? At what point do we say enough is enough and contact social care, or go to court?

The answer to all of these questions is if and when what the parents are doing, or not doing, starts to have a negative impact on the child, this is when we need to act. This is when the health visitor, the GP, the dentist, the nursery worker, the school, the college need to start talking to the parents, or a referral needs to be made to social care, depending on the severity of the problem.

Case example: When to intervene

When Sarah started school there were some concerns about her appearance. She was often a bit grubby and a bit unkempt. Her hair was rarely brushed, and one of her shoes had holes in it. She also had head lice.

Sarah had a sunny disposition and made friends quickly. The teachers kept an eye on things and she seemed to be fine.

After the Christmas holidays Sarah came back to school. The next term she seemed to become dirtier and the head lice became more prolific. She was starting to smell. The teachers noticed other children were starting to avoid her, and parents were drawing their children away from her in the playground. Sarah was becoming more withdrawn, she was also constantly scratching her head, and was finding it hard to concentrate.

At this point the school approached the parents and shared their concerns about Sarah. The parents were extremely hostile in their response. The school knew they had to do something because the neglect was having an impact on Sarah. They discussed the situation with the school nurse, and agreed that she would have a chat with Sarah. This she did, and during the conversation Sarah told her that 'Mummy is sad' and 'Daddy shouts'.

At this point the professionals felt they needed some advice, so they contacted social care with all the information they had. The point is that they acted correctly. When Sarah's presentation started to have a negative impact on her, they did something about it.

REMEMBER...

When the parent is doing something that is having a negative impact on the physical or emotional development of the child, this is when professionals need to intervene.

An easy dilemma to look at is the state of the home – what is 'good enough'? Am I judging the family harshly because I would not live like that, but it is alright for me, because I am not in an abusive relationship, and my partner does not drink, and we are both earning a salary, so we are very lucky? Go back to 'What is the impact on the child?' If the 18-month-old is picking out cigarette ends from the ashtray and chewing them, if he is getting into the cat litter tray, if there is animal faeces in the garden and he is now crawling out there, if there is broken glass all around the bin, then he is going to be adversely affected by those things. If everything is dirty and greasy and the floor has not been cleaned for weeks but there are no immediate dangers, I would be thinking more, as I would in the other scenarios as well, about why that was. A home in that state will tell you about the parents' mental health and emotional wellbeing. Although the state of the home is a symptom, and not the cause, it is nonetheless a clue that should tell you that all is not well.

It is the cumulative effect of neglect that does most of the damage, and this is increasingly being understood. In the 2013 version of statutory guidance, *Working Together to Safeguard Children*,[11] it specifically makes reference to the need to act in a timely way in neglect cases: 'Practitioners should be rigorous in assessing and monitoring children at risk of neglect to ensure they are adequately safeguarded over time. They should act decisively to protect the child by initiating care proceedings where existing interventions are insufficient.' The current emphasis is very much on being proactive and not allowing drift in cases, just as the time expected for care proceedings to take has been reduced from 40 to 26 weeks. It is all about tackling delay because what delay actually means is that children's outcomes are being affected – every day is another day of uncertainty and/or maltreatment for that child.

Neglect and adolescents

Myth: 'Neglect only affects babies and young children'

Neglect affects children throughout their entire childhood and into early adulthood.

Many of our services are focused on very young children, and this is for a number of reasons. First of all, it is this age group that is the most vulnerable, in terms of being at greatest risk of death from maltreatment. As a 2011 NSPCC report says, 'On average, the under ones are eight times more likely to be killed than older children, and nearly half of all serious case reviews

---

11   Department for Education (2013) *Working Together to Safeguard Children: A Guide to Inter-Agency Working to Safeguard and Promote the Welfare of Children.* London: Department for Education

are in relation to babies under one year.'[12] As well as this, it is now generally accepted that 90 per cent of the brain develops before a child is five,[13] so this gives us a sense of urgency – if we can get in early enough, everything will be okay.

Relatively little is understood about the brain and how it works, but what we now know is that it is in a constant state of neuroplasticity, which means it is changing all the time. Emerging research tells us that during adolescence there are significant changes in the brain, and it is developing at a rapid rate, effectively reforming.[14] What this means is that the adolescent can be as affected by neglect as a three-year-old. It also means that there should always be optimism. As things can change for the worse, so things can change for the better. The work that is done with adolescents is as vital as the work done with young children. We will look further at this in the section Working with teenagers in Chapter 6.

Over the last few years there has been increasing recognition of child sexual exploitation. This is explored further in Chapter 6, but in the recent Independent Inquiry into Child Sexual Exploitation in Rotherham, over a third of the victims were known to child protection agencies.[15] Most of these were children who were thought to have 'gone off the rails'. No, these are not children who have 'gone off the rails'. These are children who are being neglected.

As children get older, they are also more likely to be affected by another type of neglect – agency neglect. This is not a type of abuse that is recognised, but it will have a negative impact on the child, just

---

12 Cuthbert, C., Rayns, G. and Stanley, K. (2011) All Babies Count. Prevention and Protection for Vulnerable Babies. London: NSPCC. Available at www.teescpp.org.uk/Websites/safeguarding/images/Documents/NSPCC-All-babies-count-research-report-nov11.pdf

13 Zero to Three (no date) 'FAQ's on the Brain.' Available at www.zerotothree.org/child-development/brain-development/faqs-on-the-brain.html

14 National Juvenile Justice Network (2012) *Using Adolescent Brain Research to Inform Policy: A Guide for Juvenile Justice Advocates.* Fact sheet. September. Available at www.njjn.org/uploads/digital-library/Brain-Development-Policy-Paper_Updated_FINAL-9-27-12.pdf

15 Jay, A. (2014) *Independent Inquiry into Child Sexual Exploitation in Rotherham (1997–2013).* Rotherham Metropolitan Borough Council. Available at www.rotherham.gov.uk/downloads/file/1407/independent_inquiry_cse_in_rotherham

as all types of abuse do. If we remove a child from their home, and then move them from one foster carer to another and another and another, and then if we put them in a Bed & Breakfast and forget all about them, and along the way they have had nine different social workers, and we have moved them around the country and made them change schools nine times, we are repeating the neglect they suffered at the hands of their parents. There are many challenges in working with adolescents; we cannot 'do' to them as we 'do' to little children. We cannot tell them where they must live, or dictate what they do, but that should never mean that we turn a blind eye to their vulnerabilities and their needs and only judge them on their behaviour, rather than look at what has contributed to that.

When I was describing neglect at the beginning of this chapter, I described it as an act of omission by the parent. This is not necessarily the case with adolescents – sometimes it can be an act of commission, a deliberate act – for example, the parents who throw their child out of home, or the parents who leave without telling their child.

Case example: Neglect of adolescents

I was working with a young person who had a very difficult relationship with her mother. One day she got back home and her mother and her younger siblings had gone, and all their belongings had gone too. There was no note, and when she rang her mum's phone, she was told that the number did not exist. The mother had disappeared without a trace. This was in the south east of England, and she eventually found out that her mother had gone to live with a man she had met who lived in Glasgow. She tracked her down, but her mother said she did not want anything to do with her, and that she was not welcome in her house.

It is impossible to imagine what that must have felt like to that young person. Unsurprisingly, she went completely off the rails, and her behaviour became more and more extreme and harder and harder to deal with. We had to keep reminding ourselves why she was behaving the way she was. There cannot be many greater traumas for a child than their being rejected by a parent.

Evidencing neglect

Myth: 'Neglect is the hardest category to evidence'

This seems to be generally accepted view by professionals who want social care to become involved with a family and with social workers who are going to court. I myself said it for many years, as a frontline social worker, but now I have changed my view. For the last eight years, part of the work I do has included serious case reviews and other consultancy work. Now being on the other side, what I see is that we very often do not present the evidence, and then we criticise social care, or the court, for not accepting our professional opinion.

Case example: Evidencing neglect

A school had had a battle with social care for eight months over a family that the school strongly believed were neglecting their children. The school thought that these children should be made the subject of child protection plans because, in their view, they were suffering significant harm as a result of neglect. For eight months social care resisted and said that they thought the best way to meet these children's needs was through the common assessment framework (CAF). After many testy conversations, and at the end of her tether, the head teacher said to the social work manager, 'But we've been buying their uniform for the last two years!' The social work manager asked if the duty team knew that, and the head teacher said, 'No. It's just what we do.'

It turned out that when the school had spoken to the mother about the importance of school uniform, the mother said she could not afford it, but she could afford to buy cigarettes and alcohol. This is all part of the evidence. If you believe a child needs a service, you have to evidence your argument.

This brings me on to my pet peeve, which I write and speak about regularly – the use of the words 'inappropriate' and 'appropriate'. The amount of times I read in a report the word 'inappropriate'...

They mean absolutely nothing at all because they are judgements, and so they have different meaning for each of us. If I tell you a child was using inappropriate language, what does that mean to you? What would you imagine that language to be? To some it would be blaspheming, to others it would be a lot more. The point is, that it means nothing.

I read many court papers now and am unsurprised that the judge refuses an application to remove the child because the evidence is not there to support the application. Then I read the files and there is so much evidence – if it had only been presented factually and clearly, there may well have been a different outcome.

Case example: 'Inappropriate' behaviour

I recently did a review of a young man who had been charged with a serious sexual offence. The London borough wanted to examine whether this could have been predicted and/or prevented. The young man had been identified as having special educational needs from a young age, so there was an abundance of educational psychologist reports. I read every one. Each one made several references to 'inappropriate sexualised behaviour', 'inappropriate language' and 'inappropriate sexual language'. There were no details, and by the time I had read every single one of those reports, I was none the wiser as to how this young man had spoken and behaved as he had grown up. It was deeply frustrating.

The same is true of 'appropriate': 'The mother responded appropriately to her baby.' What does that mean? We need to be very specific and spell out what is happening, what we are seeing, what is being said, what we are concerned about – not couch it in all-consuming words that mean nothing. In your referral/report, say that the mother always made eye contact with her baby, she responded every time her baby 'cooed', she was very attentive to her baby's needs, when her baby got fractious she talked to her and jiggled her around and pointed things out to her. Paint a picture of what you have seen.

REMEMBER...
Please do not use the words 'appropriate' and 'inappropriate' because they are a judgement, and so mean different things to different people.

When you are considering whether you think a child is being neglected, have the courage of your convictions, based on what you have seen and what you know. Too often we wait for a medical expert to tell us there is no organic reason why a child is not walking, when they are three years old. We wait for the specialist to tell us the child has delayed speech, when the child is five, but we know perfectly well that the reason the child is not talking is because no one ever talks to the child. Of course there are children with disabilities who have delayed development, and a diagnosis may not be made until the child is of school age, but if you are working with babies and young children, and a baby/child seems to be doing something much later than everyone else, or not at all, ask yourself why. Is there anything about the home environment that concerns you? Do you think there is an environmental reason why that child is not developing? Children only develop through our encouragement. Babies learn to talk and to walk because we encourage them. Most of the children who lie in cots in institutions throughout the world, who have been there since they were babies, will not have been born with disabilities – they have become disabled because no one ever encouraged them to develop.

Case example: Evidence of neglect

I was visiting a family whose five children were all the subject of child protection plans because of neglect. When I arrived, the six-month-old baby was lying in her pram. She was feeding herself with a bottle. I ended up being in the home for an hour-and-a-half, and during that time many people came and went, including uniformed police, and there was a lot of screaming, shouting and crying. During that hour-and-a-half the baby fed herself until she fell asleep. After about 20 minutes she woke up again. She felt round for the bottle and carried on feeding herself until she was sucking on air. She then dropped the bottle and just lay there. Throughout all of that time, she did not make a squeak.

That baby knew there was no point making any noise because no one would respond. There is the evidence of neglect.

When you are trying to evidence the neglect you believe the child is suffering, it helps to break it down. Neglect is such a huge area and a broad spectrum. Different researchers talk about different types of neglect, but broadly you can break it down into six categories: physical, emotional, medical, nutritional, educational, and lack of supervision and guidance.

The sooner children receive the additional support they need, the greater their chances. Every child deserves that.

What the research tells us

There is a wealth of research that has built up over the last 40 years or so. The current thinking that is informing policy and practice is that 80 per cent of the brain has developed by the time a child is three, and 90 per cent by the time the child is five, as set out earlier. Therefore, although the brain is in a constant stage of neuroplasticity, which means it is changing all the time, it is essential that we intervene early, for the sake of the child. Neuroscience is a relatively new science, and is constantly being questioned and challenged. What is unarguable, however, is that neglect has a devastating impact on a child's life.

Neglect is a factor in 60 per cent of serious case reviews, and was a factor in 11 of the 14 child suicides that led to a serious case review.[16] In extreme cases, neglect kills children. These cases are most likely to be accidental overlay, or an accident when the parent is under the influence of a substance. We respond differently as professionals to injuries that are the result of physical abuse than

---

16 Brandon, M., Sidebotham, P., Bailey, S., Belderson, P., Hawley, C., Ellis, C. and Megson, M. (2012) *New Learning from Serious Case Reviews: A Two Year Report for 2009–11*. London: Department for Education. Available at www.gov.uk/government/uploads/system/uploads/attachment_data/file/184053/DFE-RR226_Report.pdf

if they are the result of a lack of supervision. If a three-year-old is beyond parental control and is continually running into the road, and then one day gets hit by a car and is killed, the impact for the child is the same as if the parent/carer actually put that child in the middle of the road. The same is true for the baby that is continuously left unsupervised on the bed, who keeps falling on its head. The end result is no different than if the parent is deliberately dropping the baby on its head. Our first thought should always be, 'What is the impact on the child?'

We know from research and serious case reviews that what we are prone to do with neglect cases is to look at incidents in isolation, and what we really need to do is consider the cumulative effect of all of the incidents. And the most effective way we can do that is by using multi-agency chronologies that help us to build up a pattern of behaviour. (I say more about multi-agency chronologies in Chapter 7.)

We know that there are close links made between neglect and attachment theory. What attachment theory and research offer us is a useful framework for understanding the dynamics of maltreatment, and why it is so often passed from one generation to the next. The thinking is that if the primary care giver can create a loving, stress-free environment and can prioritise her baby's needs above her own, the baby's nervous system becomes securely attached. What this results in are children who are self-confident, trusting, hopeful, and able to deal with conflict and stress. They feel safe and are able to balance their emotions, make sense of their lives, and create positive expectations of relationships.

A secure attachment also builds resilience in children, and resilience is vital because it gives children the ability to not only deal with challenges effectively, but also to bounce back from them, strengthened and more resilient. Resilience also gives children a secure base and good self-esteem, which matters so much because if you value yourself, you value what others do to you, and you think you are worth something. You can make something of your life and will be treated well because you believe that is your right. How many children do we work with who seem to have an internal model of powerlessness? They have a complete lack of belief in self-efficacy, that they can sort problems out for themselves. The trouble is, that if you grow up believing that, it is then easy to blame everyone else for everything that happens because you feel you have no control over your life.

It is important to bear in mind that none of this is clear cut. There are many factors that affect children's development, including whether there is anyone else in their life who is emotionally available to them, but if children have lived with severe neglect and there has been no one else to nurture them, they will be the opposite of those described above.

Here is a brief summary from the NSPCC of the different types of attachment you may see, but remember that any diagnosis should only be made by an expert:

Mary Ainsworth translated attachment theory into practice, developing the strange situation procedure, a clinical assessment devised to measure how infants respond to the experience of separation from their mother.

Securely attached infants are confident their mothers will be emotionally available. The secure infant becomes distressed during separation in the strange situation, and seeks contact with the mother on their return. The infant is able to be comforted by the mother. Securely attached children generally have better social skills and are more empathetic and responsive.

In *avoidant attachments* the child shows little, if any, distress at the parent's departure during the strange situation procedure, and on the parent's return they avoid close contact, seeming to prefer playing on their own. Attachment theory explains this behaviour as the consequence of consistent rejection by the parent, particularly at times when the infant showed distress. As a result, the child has no confidence that when they seek care they will receive a helpful response.

Insecure-ambivalent attachment is characterised by the infant becoming extremely distressed at the parent's departure in the strange situation procedure, but remaining inconsolable when the parent returns. The theory here is that these infants have experienced unreliable or inconsistent care from the parent, leaving them feeling anxious about the parent's availability, and that the expression of their needs has to be maximised in order to get a response.

Insecure-disorganised attachment refers to the bizarre behaviours (including momentary freezing) shown by some children on their mother's return in the strange situation procedure. This behaviour is thought to be the consequence of the infant's exposure to frightening or inexplicable behaviour on the part of the parent, who is also, paradoxically, the person on whom the infant depends.[17]

Minnesota Longitudinal study of Parents and Children[18]

I want to end this chapter with a summary of an ongoing research project called the Minnesota Longitudinal Study of Parents and Children.

The reason why I have chosen this study over all the research in the field of neglect is because it encompasses much of the other mainstream research around the impact of neglect. I have not come across other neuroscientists who challenge the findings of this study.

The study started in America in 1975. It is a longitudinal study that has followed a sample of 267 children since then. All of the children were born to mothers identified as being at risk of parenting problems due to unstable life circumstances, youth, poverty, lack of support and low education. A major focus of the project has been on the antecedents of abuse and neglect, so what causes it, as well as the long-term consequences of maltreatment

---

17 Cuthbert, C., Rayns, G. and Stanley, K. (2011) All Babies Count. Prevention and Protection for Vulnerable Babies. London: NSPCC. Available at www. teescpp.org.uk/Websites/safeguarding/images/Documents/NSPCC-All-babies-count-research-report-nov11.pdf

18 See www.cehd.umn.edu/icd/research/parent-child/

on children's development. The children were identified as suffering physical abuse, physical neglect and emotional neglect.

What this project has found encompasses much of the other mainstream research around the impact of neglect, and so I will summarise it here.

What the research found was that at age one, two thirds of the neglected children had an anxious or insecure attachment to their primary carer – the child was highly dependent on, but unable to be soothed by, their primary carer. If you think of this in practical terms, it means a very difficult baby to care for. For most parents, when their baby cries, they pick the baby up and the baby stops crying. This is a deeply satisfying feeling, that they have made everything alright, but if parents pick their baby up because all the professionals keep telling them that they have to, but the baby keeps screaming, what is the incentive? Why would they pick the baby up?

At age two, the neglected children were easily frustrated, non-compliant and displayed considerable anger, again, a very hard child to look after.

At three-and-a-half, the neglected children displayed poor impulse control, rigidity, a lack of creativity and more unhappiness than any of the other groups, so parenting that child becomes even harder. Most two-year-olds are not rigid; they are easily diverted. Two of them might desperately want the red tractor, but it is usually very easy to persuade one of them that they want the blue one instead because it is so much better. The average child will move on, but this child will not; he is fixed on that red tractor and nothing else will do.

Case example: Diverting young children

I was on a bus recently going down Regent Street in London, where the toy store Hamleys is. On the bus were two children aged about three. They were very excited about seeing 'Hamaleys', as they called it, and there was a big build-up until they saw it. Then the bus continued, and after a couple of minutes one child said to the other, 'I saw Hamaleys first.' You could see the other one's brain whirring, and she said, 'I saw Hamaleys first!' This quickly descended into a passionate, heart-felt and desperately important argument until the mother said, after a couple of minutes, 'Look at the pigeons over there' and Hamaleys was all but forgotten.

Creativity in children is such an important part of their development, but it is also important for primary carers because it gives them a bit of a break. If the child will happily build a tower or draw a picture, they actually have a couple of minutes to put the washing on, or start getting the tea without any 'help'. The child who does not know how to be creative will find it hard to play alone and is more likely to need attention all the time.

At four-and-a-half, neglected children displayed poor impulse control, extreme dependence on their teachers and general maladjustments in the classroom. Teachers often speak of the child who is glued to their side all day.

What the researchers say is,

> In many ways our study shows the consequences of emotional neglect to be even more profound than physical neglect, or other types of maltreatment. At four and a half their nervous signs, self-abusive behaviour and other behaviours are all considered to be signs of psychopathology, mental ill-health.
>
> Although the maltreatment the emotionally neglected children suffered was the most subtle of all the groups, the consequences for the children were the most striking.[19]

Then, as the children grew up, the prognoses for them became even bleaker. As they became older, the neglected children were more socially withdrawn, unpopular with their peers, and became more aggressive and less attentive. They performed significantly lower than their peers academically – only five per cent were not receiving some level of special education.

When they became adolescents, the children whose primary carer was psychologically unavailable, in other words, was not there for the child, emotionally or psychologically, scored highly in terms

---

19 Sroufe, L. A., Egeland, B., Carlson, E. A. and Collins, W. A. (2009) *The Development of the Person: The Minnesota Study of Risk and Adaptation from Birth to Adulthood.* New York: Guilford Press.

of delinquency, aggression and social problems, and were more likely to attempt suicide than all the other groups.

At age 17-and-a-half, 90 per cent of the maltreated children received a diagnosis of mental illness. The highest rate was the 'psychologically unavailable' group in which all but one child received a diagnosis of at least one psychiatric disorder, and 73 per cent were diagnosed with two disorders or more, which is reflected when we look at users of adult mental health services, many of whom have been maltreated as children.

It was the physically neglected children who had the highest rates of school drop-out and academic failure, which makes complete sense because if you are dirty and smelly, who is going to want to be your friend? On top of that, if you do not have the right uniform, clothes or shoes, you are different again. The easiest and most understandable thing to do is to walk away.

The project concluded that it was maltreatment in the early years that had devastating consequences for the children's overall functioning in adolescence.

The researchers also looked at the cycle of abuse and the antecedents of abuse. This was around maltreatment generally, not specifically neglect. They found that 40 per cent of the mothers who were maltreated during their own childhood abused or neglected their children in their early years, and a further 30 per cent were borderline cases.

They concluded that there are four main ways in which a mother can break the cycle. They are:

> The presence of a loving, supportive adult during childhood. This might be a grandparent, an uncle, or an aunt – having someone who puts you first can make a huge difference to the child.

> A supportive partner at the time they become parents.

> Therapeutic interventions that enabled mothers to come to see resolution to their early issues, and achieve greater emotional stability and maturity. It is only in recent years that projects in the UK have sprung up that are working

with women who have multiple children removed, to try to help them resolve what their need is, to try to break this cycle of neglect.

> The mother's integration of the experiences of maltreatment into a coherent view of self. What this means is that some mothers and fathers, too, can just break the cycle.

Case example: Breaking the cycle of abuse

The midwife informed us that a mother who was very well known to social care was pregnant again. She had had five children, including twins, by three different partners. All of the children had been adopted. The mother had grown up in an abusive home and had witnessed domestic abuse and alcohol abuse. All of her partners had been abusive towards her, and she had been misusing alcohol, as a way of coping with her life. One of her ex-partners was in prison for armed robbery and assault.

My first thought was we would be straight into court; this would be clear-cut because of her past, but then I went to meet her and her new partner. It turned out that she was now with someone who was not violent. He was extremely loving towards her, and she no longer drank. He did not drink alcohol either. As well as this, he was very close to his aunt, and she wanted to help and support them in every way she could. His family had no history of involvement with social care.

We had a pre-birth child protection conference and all agreed that we thought they should be able to take the baby home. We put a very tight support package in place, with daily visits, including the partner's aunt and other family members, who were very supportive of them too. The couple kept the baby, and after supporting them for six months after the birth, social care closed the case.

So, as you come to the end of this chapter, please remember that neglect is just as damaging as other types of maltreatment; it affects children of all ages, and we must always act if we think a child is being neglected.

Chapter 7 looks at additional ways that we can work more constructively and effectively with families.

2 Communicating with Children

Somewhere along the way we have lost sight of the child. We have become so consumed and overwhelmed by bureaucracy, so absorbed by the needs of parents/carers, and in some cases so overwhelmed by the chaos, the hostility, the snarling dog, the domestic abuse, the drugs, the alcohol, the mental ill health (all the adult 'problems' that impact on children) that we forget about the child. All that is very understandable, but this is an opportunity to take a step back and remind ourselves why we are there.

How can we effectively assess a situation if this does not include spending time with the child? We can tick a box saying 'Child seen', but what does that mean? It means nothing, unless we have actually taken the time to see what is going on from the child's point of view. I have lost count of the number of times I have heard social workers say, 'I just don't have the time to sit down individually with all the children on my caseload.' We work in *children's* services. If we do not have the time to spend with children, then something has gone very wrong.

It is for workers at every level to insist that we cannot do our work properly unless we take the time to put ourselves in the children's shoes, to understand what it is like for them, and we can only do that by spending time with the children, talking to them, listening to them and playing with them. We should be spending at least as much time with them as with the adults. When I think back on my practice, I remember too many visits where I probably spent 50 minutes with the mother, hearing about her life, and then ten minutes at the end with the child. It should really be the other way round, and particularly with older children.

To talk with a reluctant 16-year-old, however, requires different skills from communicating with a six-month-old baby. One of the challenges in writing about communicating with children is the difference in how they communicate at different ages. I have chosen to break it down into only three main age groups, birth to five pre-school, 5–11 and 12–17, and yet the differences within each age range are vast. We must also bear in mind that children do not always follow the same path in their development, and not every child will fit neatly into the expectations of their biological age bracket. When you start working with a child of a particular age, make sure you understand what developmental stage they, generally speaking, should have reached.

In 2011 a report entitled *'Don't Make Assumptions.' Children and Young People's Views of the Child Protection System and Messages for Change*[1] was commissioned by the Office of the Children's Commissioner. These are some of the things the children said:

I don't like people looking down on me and I don't like people looking up at me like I'm an adult. I like people talking to me for my age.

Kids aren't as naïve as you think. I think the reason that people don't listen to kids is that they're kids.

Listen to what children have got to say and work with them.

Take what the young people say seriously.

I'd like to be less kept in the dark, explain things a bit more.

Be nice and don't involve your personal life. Have a general chat about stuff before going into heavy questions.

1   Cossar, J., Brandon, M. and Jordan, P. (2011) *'Don't Make Assumptions.' Children's and Young People's Views of the Child Protection System and Messages for Change*. London and Norwich: Office of the Children's Commissioner and Centre for Research on the Child and Family, University of East Anglia. Available at www.childrenscommissioner.gov.uk/force_download. php?fp=%2Fclient_assets%2Fcp%2Fpublication%2F486%2FChildrens_ and_young_peoples_views_of_the_child_protection_system_.pdf

Give children your mobile number so they can text. They might not always want to have someone talk back to them straight away.

Don't make assumptions about my thoughts and feelings.

Words of wisdom from children, and words we should all take heed of.

General rules in communicating with children of any age

There are many rules that apply regardless of the age, ethnicity or ability of the child you are working with. First of all, though, beware of making assumptions. Make sure your understanding of what the child is saying is correct and you have not leapt to conclusions.

Never use jargon. Use clear, straightforward language to explain who you are and what is happening, and, as I say elsewhere (see Chapter 1), never use the words 'appropriate' and 'inappropriate'.

Always be as honest as you can with children, but tailor your honesty so that it is right for their age, level of understanding and situation. A 13-year-old once said to a colleague of mine, 'I'm a child. I'm not thick.' I admired my colleague for telling us, and it made all of us in the team reflect on how we talk to children. Never make promises, or give reassurances you may not be able to keep.

Some children can be very difficult to talk to. Older children may be as hostile or as aggressive as an adult, and it is a natural response to avoid the challenging situation, so again, the voice of the child is overlooked.

Case example: Engaging with the child

When I was a newly qualified social worker, many years ago, I was allocated a case, a family consisting of a single mother with a 13-year-old boy, Johnie. Johnie was not attending school; his behaviour towards his mother was abusive, and he was increasingly putting himself in risky situations, by staying out at night. His father was not around, and the only other adult in his life was his maternal grandmother, to whom he was also starting to become abusive. Johnie was beyond parental control. The Child and Adolescent Mental Health Service would not become involved because his situation was not serious enough, so it was given to me. The case had been open and closed to social care many times over the years. We put another child in need plan in place, and it was not considered that there should be a child protection plan. Part of the plan was that I would visit once a week. My visits followed the same path, each week. The mother would want to use all of my time, telling me how desperate the situation was, how frightened she felt and how she needed help, all of which were very real concerns. Sometimes the grandmother was there too, and I would hear the same from her. These women had no idea what to do to bring back their child to some level of control, and to be brutally honest, neither did I. The mother had done several parenting courses over the years, none of which seemed to have made any impact on her ability to control her son. She was floundering, and so were the professionals.

Usually when I visited, Johnie would make sure he was not there, but when he was, I would attempt to talk to him. He absolutely did not want to talk to me, and to be perfectly frank, I don't blame him. I was newly qualified, I really did not know what I was doing, and I could not find a way to get him to open up. So what could I do?

We all agreed that Johnie might find it easier to build a relationship with a male worker,* who would be able to be a positive male role model for him. We brought someone in, and sure enough, Johnie was much happier, and over the next few months they built a good bond and progress was made. Johnie ended up going back to school, and with the male worker working with Johnie, and me working with the mother and grandmother, we were able to help them put in rules and boundaries that were realistic, that Johnie would adhere to, and that would keep him and them safe.

*Note: Sometimes you have to admit that someone else may be able to do a better job than you, and because of their sex, age, role etc., they may be more likely to be able to build a bond with the child, but these decisions should be made on a case by case basis. It is not as simple as 'Well he's a boy, so he needs a male worker'.

What we need to do is look behind the hostility, the aggression – keep asking yourself why that child is behaving the way they are.

There will always be a reason, as there is for the way we all behave. (For example, just today, my teenage son sent me a text asking me how my day is going. In all his years he has never been remotely interested in how my day is going, but his birthday is coming up, and he really wants a new mobile – the change in behaviour can be explained!)

Seeing children alone

There is a lot of confusion about this. Legally we cannot insist on seeing a child alone, but again, it goes back to 'How can we make a true assessment without speaking to the child?' When we visit, parents/carers may initially understandably not want their child taken off by a stranger. We need to build up trust with the parents/carers and most importantly, with the child. We need to be respectful and sometimes assertive, but there is no excuse for not seeing a child alone in the course of our work, even when we are doing preliminary investigations. Of course there will be exceptions to this when we start working with a family. For example, most young children are naturally wary of strangers, and it may be frightening for them to insist that we see them alone.

The question should be, 'Why is the parent refusing to allow us to see the child alone?' If this is the case, then this forms part of the assessment of risk. It might be that their reasons are entirely legitimate – they do not want some stranger taking their child off on their own; do not always assume their intentions are sinister. We need to be clear with parents that we cannot insist on it, but we would be concerned if they were preventing us from spending time with their children.

Non-verbal communication

We know that a high percentage of all communication is non-verbal. So we, as practitioners, need to be aware of this. Non-verbal communication includes our facial expressions, posture, gestures, tone of voice and eye contact. (Again, be careful of making assumptions based on your own culture. Within the white, British culture, children are taught that you must look at someone when you are talking to them, and that it is rude not to do so, but within some cultures it is disrespectful for a child to look an adult in the eye.) Non-verbal messages we give and receive play just as big a part in how we communicate with others as verbal messages. It is as important that we observe and learn from these, as well as from the verbal communication we have with children. What we learn from all forms of communication should form part of our assessment.

So when you are going to see that recalcitrant teenager who tells you to 'F*** off' every time you see him, make a conscious effort to ensure your body language does not tell him you are dreading this meeting. Make sure your body language is open and you are not hunched forward, with your arms wrapped round yourself. If you present this way, he will pick up on it and this will not be a good start.

Think, too, about how the child responds to you as well as the non-verbal clues they give.

Communicating with pre-school children

This is the period in a child's life when their development should be the most dramatic. When working with pre-school children, we need to be constantly asking ourselves, 'Is this normal?' 'Is this right?', and seeking specialist help if we are not sure. We cannot all be experts in everything, but there will always be people who have the knowledge we do not.

There are many ways we can communicate with a baby or young child, and many ways that they can communicate with us. We must be careful not to assume that because a baby/child is non-verbal they have nothing to tell us. This is not the case, although I knew of a mother who said to her social worker, 'Why would I talk to my baby? He can't talk.'

The difference between a newborn baby and a five-year-old is considerable, and every child progresses at a different rate. There are many books on child development. It is generally accepted that, as a rule, babies from around the age of one month start cooing.

From three months they start to take it in turns during 'conversations', for example, a mother telling her baby it is bath time. The baby responds with 'dadadadadada'. The mother waits for the child to stop, and then says something else to the baby, the baby waits, and when the mother has stopped talking, the baby responds with more babbling. The baby is learning how to communicate and the give-and-take of conversation.

From six to nine months, babies start producing more vowels and some consonants. It can take three or four months after the emergence of the first words before vocabulary increases very much, but after that, the acquisition of new words is rapid. Vocabulary typically grows from around 20 words at 18 months to around 200 words at 21 months.

At around 18 months most children start to combine single words into two-word sentences. For example, 'Mummy gone.' They will also talk about themselves in the third person, 'Mary cup', when pointing to their cup.

From the age of two, most children are uttering three or four-word sentences. They may be grammatically incorrect – 'Fishes in bowl gone' – but they can be understood.

From age three to four, speech continues to develop at a rapid pace, with the increase in vocabulary, as well as a greater improvement in understanding of grammar. Most children of three can be understood by those outside the child's circle, to some degree, even if a bit of clarification is needed sometimes!

Case example: Do not always take what young children say at face value

I used to visit a little boy called Mikey, whose best thing to do, at the age of three, was to go to the park and find sticks. He would collect all the sticks he could and then take them home. At the age of three he could not pronounce the word 'stick' but would say 'dick' instead. When I visited the home he would take me by the hand and say, 'Lady see Mikey dick.'

By the age of four, most children can be easily understood but, as always, guard against assuming you know what that child is saying if there is any chance of confusion.

Running alongside this will be the young child's willingness to talk to us – initially a stranger in the home, an outsider, who may not be very welcome, but again there are no absolutes. The 18-month-old in a happy, healthy home may be reluctant to play with, or talk to, a stranger, but the 18-month-old who lives in a house of chronic neglect may be all too willing to climb up on our knee and turn our face to theirs, while thrusting a book at us. Equally, a child living in a house full of fear and violence may be withdrawn and unwilling to talk to, or play with, a stranger. We have to judge each case on its own merit, each child on his or her own circumstances. If only it were as simple as saying, 'The first time I visited the two-year-old jumped on my knee and was stroking my face – the child must be suffering neglect, if they are like that with a complete stranger.'

How to build a relationship with the child

First of all, we must do our utmost to build a relationship with the primary carer of a very young child. We want the mother to trust us enough to let us hold her baby. If you are reading this as a social worker, be sensitive to the fact that you will probably be perceived as a threat and you will be seen to hold enormous power, although it may not feel like that to you. We must all be respectful of the child's carers.

REMEMBER...

Always ask permission to pick up a baby, or a young child. Do not presume.

I would also advise that you do not wear a strong perfume, or aftershave, when you are going to be holding someone's baby – there is nothing worse than someone handing a baby back smelling of another person's perfume.

A common way to soothe a small baby is to put our little finger in their mouth for them to suck, when we are holding them. It is an action that is very intimate, and as professionals, we should not presume to do this, unless the parent suggests it when we are holding their baby.

So, when you are working with a family with a baby, ask to hold the baby when it feels right to do so, and as the baby gets to know you, they will feel more comfortable with you. I will often hold a baby over three months old against me, but facing away from me, so they feel physically safe but they can see their primary carer. This will reassure them if they are unsure, and in time you can turn the baby round.

If you build up a relationship with a baby you will learn a lot from them, which will help strengthen your assessment. Is the baby cooing, babbling, gurgling, 'joining in' with the conversation, grabbing your finger, your pen, and responsive to you, or is the baby unresponsive and passive?

REMEMBER...

If you are going to be regularly visiting families with babies or young children, it is worth investing in a few toys yourself. You never know what you will find when you visit a home for the first time. There may be absolutely nothing. Toys you bring will provide a good distraction when you are trying to speak to the primary carer, but will also show you how a baby/young child knows how to play, in accordance with their age, and whether they are used to being given things to play with.

I am not suggesting you take a boxful, but a couple of books and a couple of baby/toddler toys will help enormously.

Once a child is able to crawl, the best way of building a relationship with them is by sitting on the floor and playing. Always let the child come to you. If you are too forward, you will frighten a child off. When you first visit a family you can be sitting talking to the adult, seeming to ignore the child, once you have said hello. That way you will not be threatening, and again, if you are visiting a home where there may be no toys, take some with you – you will need something to start building the relationship with the child and to assess how that child is. When you want to start engaging with the child, or the child shows signs of wanting to engage with you, move to sit on the floor, start playing with something, building a tower with blocks, for example, but continue talking to the primary carer. Most young children would find that hard to resist, and gradually the child will come to you. If the child is very shy, carry on talking to the adult and just pass the child a block, or put one close to them, without making eye contact. All contact must be on the child's terms and they will need to trust you. In most cases this will happen naturally over time, as long as you let the relationship develop at the child's pace. This is true of a child of any age. Follow the child's lead. Equally, though, if the child stays behind the chair all the time you are in the home, and refuses to engage with you, think about what that tells you about the child. It may be concerning, it may not. Consider all of the other factors. Regardless of a child's age, when you are making your assessment you need to know that you have done your utmost to engage with that child, and if the child will not engage with you, what is there to learn from that?

One of the difficulties of working with this age group is that, in most cases, there is unlikely to be a medical diagnosis for why a child is developmentally delayed. You have to ascertain if that under-five-year-old child is likely to still not be talking for the simple reason that no one is consistently speaking to him, or if there may be an organic reason why he is non-verbal. Always question, never assume, and always consider the context.

Even with this age group we can learn so much from the children about their lives. With this age group, play is the most effective way to communicate. A four-year-old is unlikely to sit at a table and tell you about their life, but if you have pens and paper and toys, you will learn an awful lot, but as always, you must guard against making assumptions.

Case example: Alternative ways to communicate with young children

Emily was four years old. She was very reluctant to speak. There were concerns of sexual abuse, but little evidence. One day, Emily drew a picture that was of two people, who she said were, 'Me and Daddy.' They were stick drawings, but she had drawn herself with an enormous mouth, completely disproportionate to the other facial features she had drawn, and tears coming from her eyes. She had drawn her father with a huge penis and no facial features.

You will also learn what is normal for that child. For example, if you think a three-year-old is being physically abused, when you are having your time alone with the child, play a game where someone does something naughty and then say something like, 'The Mummy teddy bear is sad that Peter teddy bear smacked his sister. Mummy teddy bear says that Peter has to go to sit at the table till dinner time', and see how the child reacts. Young children will often correct you and say that the punishment has to be whatever they have experienced. It might be the child saying, 'No. Peter has to sit on the naughty step', but it might be 'No. Mummy teddy bear beat Peter' or 'Peter is a bad boy. Peter go in cupboard.' You can test out theories through playing with the child, but as always, I would add a note of caution. It may be that that child has watched something on television, or overheard an adult conversation about other people. Don't jump to conclusions.

Case example: Don't jump to conclusions

I was working with a little boy of three who, during a visit, told me, on two occasions, that he liked 'playing with Mummy's knickers in the bath.' I was not there because of child protection concerns but still, as a social worker, this information did concern me. I asked the mother if she knew what he was referring to, and she told me it was a necklace of hers that he played with in the bath but he could not say the word 'necklace'. Just to be sure I asked her where the necklace was and she said it was in the bathroom, so I asked the little boy if he would show me the 'knickers'; I said I would love to see it. Off he went and returned with a necklace. (It had glass beads and that was why he liked playing with it in the bath because it made the beads shiny.)

A child under five will usually not understand the significance of what they are telling us. If you feel it is safe to do so, ask the primary carer, as in the case example above. Try to clarify the facts. For example, if a woman has a new partner who is considered to be a risk to children and her little girl says to you, 'Daddy put his stick in my twinkle', it is fine to ask the little girl where her 'twinkle' is and where Daddy's 'stick' is. You could draw a simple picture of a man. It might be completely innocent, but if she points to the genital area in response to both questions, you should be concerned. You may also need to try to establish who 'Daddy' is, if there may be more than one adult male in her immediate family. Once you have established those basic facts, apart from providing kindness, reassurance and asking about the child's welfare (for example, asking if anything is hurting), don't ask anything else or ask the child to repeat what she said. If it is decided that the police should video interview the child, it can be harder for them to build their case if the child has been questioned too many times previously. It is also not good for the child to be asked to repeat their experience too many times, to too many people. We must also be very careful about not asking a child any suggestive or leading questions, or doing anything else that may undermine the child's evidence in a criminal trial. And it is important to make an accurate record afterwards of the questions asked, and the answers given, as this will be important to any criminal investigation. In this case, if you had reason to believe the child had been sexually abused, there would need to be a child protection investigation which would include specially trained police officers interviewing the child as well as a medical examination.

Confidentiality

All children need to know that, in most circumstances, we cannot keep secrets. I do, however, talk about 'good secrets' with children. For example, if a four-year-old has been shopping with her daddy to buy a present for mummy's birthday and she shows you that present but tells you it is a secret, you can reinforce that that is a 'good secret'. (In my experience, parents usually know what the present is anyway, and feign surprise for their child's benefit!) It is unlikely that a child under five will have a clear understanding of the concept of secrecy and therefore tell you something and then tell you not to tell anyone, but if that does happen, and you are concerned about what they have told you, use clear and simple language to explain that you cannot keep it secret because you are worried that they, or someone else, is being hurt, and that you need to make sure everyone is safe.

Communicating with children aged 5–11

By the age of five, most English-speaking children who are verbal will be easily understood, but, as always, we must guard against assuming we know what a child means. If in doubt, ask the question. Language moves on very quickly.

Case example: Don't assume you always understand

Several years ago I was working with Josh, an 11-year-old boy whose mother was alcohol-dependent. Josh had a very close bond with his mother. He had no siblings, and his father had never been in his life. He had no grandparents, so it was just Josh and his mother. Josh's mother had been in a rehabilitation clinic and as a result, Josh had been placed in foster care. His mother had been doing very well and was about to return home, to continue her rehabilitation in the community. Josh was to be allowed unsupervised contact with her. As I was telling him this he suddenly said 'sick'. I thought that was a strange response because I thought he would be really pleased, but I carried on talking. Again he said 'sick'. I could not work it out. He looked pleased but kept saying 'sick', so I asked him what 'sick' meant. He told me that 'sick' means 'cool'!

It is important to remember that most children starting school will think that everyone else in the world lives the way they do, and it is often only if they are able to start building friendships, visiting their friends' homes and generally going out into the wider world that they start to understand that maybe not everyone else lives the way they do.

Case example: What is normal to a child

I was working with a mother who told me of her experiences of growing up. Her father had suffered from obsessive-compulsive disorder. It was in the days before this was a recognised disorder, and he was just thought to be 'a bit odd'. She was an only child, and she and her family were very isolated; she thinks parents told their children to stay away because of her father. (He used to spend a lot of time in the local supermarket, rearranging the tins so they all faced the same way.) She was 11 before she made her first real friend, whose house she started going to. She remembers the shock she felt that this family did not count up the used tea bags and keep them in piles of ten. They did not have to open packets of biscuits, crisps and other foods a certain way. She was so surprised because the father slept in a bed with the mother – her father slept in a chair because he was obsessed with the news and rarely left his chair, except to use the bathroom, when she or her mother would then have to watch for him so that they could report on what he had missed. This family that was 'normal' was abnormal to her.

The best way to find out about a child of this age's day-to-day life is to ask them, but not just sitting across a table. Be creative. You could draw a picture and write down every day of the week, and then ask which is the best day of the week and why, and draw pictures. (If you are terrible at drawing like me, that can make children laugh, but make it fun, however you do it.) You can then ask if there is a day they do not like and why. You could learn all sorts of interesting information by expanding on this – 'Can you draw a picture of who cooks the tea, and I have to guess who it is?' 'Can you draw a picture of who lives in your house?' And so on.

You also need to remember that children within this age bracket may start to become more guarded, either because they are starting to understand that what is happening in their house is not right, or because of threats, or because of an instinctive desire to protect the people they love.

Be mindful, too, of the fact that, conversely, a child may not know what is happening is wrong, for example, with some cases of sexual abuse. The research is clear that the majority of perpetrators are someone within the child's community, and many perpetrators are within the child's home.[2] If someone is a sex offender and they want to sexually abuse their child, the chances are they will not get away with raping their child day after day, but if they do it in a way that the child likes, they could get away with it for years. The harsh reality is that if someone masturbates their child and is gentle with them, it will feel nice, and how would that child ever know that it was abuse? It would just be something else they do with mummy, with daddy, like cuddling, kissing and tickling that feels nice.

So if you are working with a child in this age range and there are concerns of sexual abuse, this could be explored in a very broad way – 'Who gives the best cuddles in this house?' 'What makes Daddy's cuddles so special?' Be careful not to ask leading questions, but talking with children like this can be useful in so many ways because as well as hearing things that may deeply concern you, you may also hear things that are deeply reassuring about the parent about whom you are trying to ascertain whether they are protective, or not.

How to build a relationship with the child

It is equally as important with this age group that we build a relationship with the child's primary carer, if possible.

REMEMBER...

Social workers do not have the legal right to insist on seeing a child alone, if the parents object. However, ask yourself the question, 'Why are the parents refusing to allow it?', and that should form part of your assessment.

---

2   See www.nspcc.org.uk

(In my experience, it is unusual for parents to refuse point-blank.)

Even the younger children in this age group may very well be happy to be taken out, although I despair of social workers sitting in fast food restaurants with children – there are very few children who are comfortable sitting across the table from a stranger talking about their life. And apart from anything else, there may well be people in the restaurant the young person knows. It may be fine at the very beginning of your relationship to encourage the child out, but please find other things to do! (More on this later.)

With a younger child, follow the suggestions for the previous age group. Sit on the floor. Even with the younger ones, be honest why you are there. With a six-year-old it could be as simple as, 'I want to try to help everyone in your family be safe and everyone feel a bit happier, so I will be coming to see you and mummy/daddy for a while.' With an 11-year-old, they will most likely know what is going on in the family, and therefore you should explain that you are a social worker, if that is your role, and that social workers help families when they need a bit of extra support, or when grown-ups are worried about them. Many of the families you work with will have preconceived ideas about what social workers do (and some ideas are not even repeatable here). It is up to you to dispel those misconceptions, and just as you should explain to the adults in the family why you are involved, so you should to the child. If you have picked up on hostility in the family, or anxiety, acknowledge that with the child, rather than just contradicting what their parents have told them.

Case example: Explaining what social workers do

I was visiting the home of an 11-year-old girl, Helen, for the first time. The school had contacted social care because Helen's attendance had recently dropped off, and when she was in school, she seemed to be very tired and withdrawn. There had been ongoing concerns about her mother, Maureen's, mental ill health, which led to a belief that Helen was having to care for Maureen more and more. I knew that Helen was very protective of her mother, and when she let me in she went and sat very close to her.

The first thing I did was explain to them why I was there.

> Me: 'I have come to see you because the school is worried that you have not been in recently, Helen, and when you are there, they are worried that you seem very tired and quiet. So the school contacted social care because that is what they do when they are worried about someone at their school, and that is why I have come to see you, to see how you both are, and whether there is anything we can do to help.'

(You should have checked with other agencies before your visit to see whether they had any concerns or information that is relevant.)

At this point Maureen started crying.

> Helen: 'We are fine and everything is fine. There's nothing wrong. I just don't like school and I want to stay at home with my mum.'

> Me: 'Do you know what? Sometimes people are frightened when a social worker comes round because they think we are just here to take children away. There are lots of families, who at different times in their lives just need a bit of extra help, and social workers do lots of work like that too. I really am here to help you, but I can only do that if you can tell me how things are at the moment, for both of you.'

> Helen: 'We don't want any help. We just want to be by ourselves.'

> Me: 'And that is fine, Helen, but because we are worried about you and about your mum, I can't just go away. Maureen, can I start by asking you how you are and how things are for you at the moment?'

So I explained why I was there and what social workers do. I then had to ascertain from Maureen and Helen how things were for them, and what really happens in their home, through gentle and exploratory questions.

Children may have a very real fear that you are only there to take them away, and we need to do our upmost to dispel this myth.

The difficulty is, of course, that you cannot say that you definitely will not, depending on what you find out, and what your conclusions and those of other professionals involved are. Also bear in mind that family members may very well be telling the children not to speak to you because 'All social workers do is take children away from their parents.' In that situation, it is very confusing for children because their family is saying one thing, and you are saying another.

With any child you will need to ascertain early on the child's level of maturity, and how to effectively communicate with that individual child. Sometimes we have to ask children the most personal and difficult questions at the start of our relationship with them. It is not ideal, but some situations necessitate this. Put yourself in the child's shoes. Imagine someone knocks on your door and then starts asking you intimate questions about your life. This is what the child has to contend with. It is never as simple as just answering questions, and why would they want to anyway? This is why it is so important to try to build that rapport and trust. In the words of one child, 'You've got to trust [the social worker] and she's got to trust you. Otherwise there's no point.'[3]

Where best to see the child

This is the age group where you need to start thinking really creatively about the best place to see the child, to start building that relationship. With most children, the best place to start is in the home, but as they start to trust you, and depending on the circumstances at home, you may well learn more from them and build a better relationship if you go out. The home may feel a very unsafe place for that child, and you can create a safe environment in your car, or somewhere else. In my view this is the age range when

---

3   Cossar, J., Brandon, M. and Jordan, P. (2011) 'Don't Make Assumptions.'
    Children's and Young People's Views of the Child Protection System and Messages
    for Change. London and Norwich: Office of the Children's Commissioner
    and Centre for Research on the Child and Family, University of East
    Anglia. Available at www.childrenscommissioner.gov.uk/force_download.
    php?fp=%2Fclient_assets%2Fcp%2Fpublication%2F486%2FChildrens_
    and_young_peoples_views_of_the_child_protection_system_.pdf

the car really comes into its own. It is much easier for most children to talk when they are not face-to-face. I have had more children disclose information to me in my car than anywhere else. And I will always go the long way round, so that we get more time in the car.

When children start to become more aware, they may well not want you to go and see them at school, or be noticeable if you pick them up from school. Most children do not want people asking questions about who you are and why they have got a social worker. Work out with the child what they want to say if someone asks them who you are.

It is easier in the summer because you can go to a park; you can feed the ducks, go on the swings, but again, go to a park where the child will not know anyone, so they are not embarrassed by having 'a worker'. If you are working with a ten-year-old who thinks feeding the ducks is far too childish, take a blanket and a pack of cards, or a couple of bats and a ball. Put a few good, interactive games on your tablet or your phone. This is how children build relationships, through play.

In the winter you can always drive to one of those big pet stores and go and look at the pets and the fish. Do your talking in the car, go the long way round, and leave time in the store for just enjoying looking at the animals and fish. With older children you could make it a game, guessing how many guinea pigs there will be next week when you go, how many hamsters etc. It will be more interesting for a ten-year-old than sitting in a fast food restaurant, and you will learn an awful lot more.

How to respond to a child making a disclosure

Within this age range children may start to understand the significance of what they are telling you, so you will need to handle the situation very sensitively.

The most important thing to remember is that our starting point should always be to believe the child. We hear too often of children who have told someone about the abuse that is being done to them, and they have not been believed. If that child has been brave enough to tell you what is happening, it is vital they feel they are believed. Of course there will be some situations where the child has got confused about something, or is not telling the truth, but we can find that out later. To begin with we must show that child that we believe them.

Listen to the child without interrupting them. If they become upset when they are telling you, comfort them, but I would not do more than put a hand on their shoulder. If they are disclosing sexual abuse, I would not touch them, but you will have to gauge the level of comfort with each child. When they have finished, reassure them by telling them they have done the right thing in telling you. Tell them they are brave/clever, but do not patronise them. As one child said, 'I am a child. I am not thick.'

Keep calm and try not to show your distress if they are telling you something terrible. Showing sympathy and/or empathy is essential, but crying is best avoided, if you possibly can – I find digging my nails in the palms of my hands works well if I think I am going to cry.

Confidentiality

If a child starts a sentence with, 'What would you do if I told you a secret but you can't tell anyone?', I would say something like, 'The only secrets I can keep are nice secrets, like, if you were going to tell me what you had bought your mum for Christmas. But if you were going to tell me something about someone not being safe, then I could not keep that secret. Do you want to tell me and then we can talk about whether that can be a secret or not?'

Be clear with children that you cannot keep this particular secret while continually reinforcing that they have done the right thing by telling you. Be as clear and as honest as you can be about what is likely to happen next.

Case example: Being honest

I was working with a mother who had three girls under the age of eight. She had a history of relationships with men who were considered to be a risk to children. Her latest partner, Tom, who was not the father of any of the girls, was on the sex offender register. He had convictions for sexually abusing young girls. The girls were all subject to child protection plans because of the risk of sexual abuse. The mother had agreed to end the relationship with Tom. The child protection plan had a contingency that if he was seen in the home, social care would apply to the court for emergency protection orders. Because of the mother's history, there were grave concerns about whether she would protect her children. All of the agencies were on high alert.

One day I got a call from the eight-year-old, Martha's, school, telling me that Martha had told her teacher that Tom came for tea last night and stayed the night with mummy, and 'he's not allowed'. The teacher had, quite rightly, clarified that this is the Tom everyone is so concerned about, and then did not say any more to Martha but rang me, as the social worker.

It was agreed that I would go to the school and I talk to Martha with the teacher attending. Martha had a close bond with her teacher, and we knew it would be reassuring for her to have her there. Just before I arrived, the teacher called Martha in to just explain that I was coming to see her, to see how things were, and she reassured Martha that she was not in any trouble.

The conversation went something like this:

Me: 'Hello Martha. I've come to see you today to see how you are and to talk about Mummy and Tom. You're not in any trouble, Martha and Mrs X, the teacher, tells me you did a beautiful painting today!'

Me: 'I just needed to come and see you because of what you told Mrs X about tea yesterday. Can you tell me who came for tea yesterday?'

Martha: 'Tom did.'

Me: 'Martha, how long did Tom stay for, can you remember?'

Martha: 'He stayed the night with Mummy in Mummy's bed but Mummy said he had to go before the neighbours saw him, so he had to go before breakfast when it was still dark.'

Me: 'Is Tom allowed to stay at your house?'

Martha: 'No.'

Me: 'Do you remember why, Martha?'

Martha: 'You said because sometimes he isn't kind to children, and you said no one was allowed to touch me and my sisters in our private parts, except if Mummy is helping us. But Mummy said you are wrong and Tom is kind. She said if I told you, you would take us away from Mummy, but I didn't tell you, I told Mrs X.'

Me: 'Yes, Martha and you were very clever to tell Mrs X because the most important thing is that you and your sisters are safe, but Mrs X had to tell me because she has to make sure you are safe, just like I do. So what's going to happen now is that you can go and have your dinner and I am going to go back to my office. We will decide how we can keep you and your sisters safe, and then we will tell you what is going to happen. Is that okay? Is there anything you want to ask me or Mrs X about?'

Ideally, once you have the emergency protection orders, you should be the one to go back to Martha and take her to her placement, but don't promise Martha she will go back to school because you cannot guarantee that. It may be that she has to be placed far away and, although every effort is made to keep a child at their school when they are placed in care, it is not always practical. Wherever Martha and her sisters go she will need constant reassurance that she did a very brave thing and she has made sure her sisters are safe.

In my experience, children are often more protective of other children, particularly younger siblings, than they are of themselves, and they generally understand if you explain that you have to do something to make sure their little sisters/brothers are safe. This is often why they have disclosed in the first place.

Communicating with children aged 12–17

If any child really feels they have been listened to, and that their views have been given consideration, they are more likely to accept the plan we want to put in place. Of course in some instances the child will be violently opposed to the plan, but that should only mean that we work harder at our relationship with them, trying to get them to understand why it is we want to do the things we want to do as well as listening to their views. And our best chance of affecting positive change with this age group depends on how we communicate with them.

The other thing we need to remember when working with this age group is that they will have a much greater understanding of the possible consequences/ramifications of what they tell us, and may therefore be, understandably, much more guarded.

Case example: Deciding to 'tell'

I was working with a mother, Louise, who was on a methadone programme. She had a long history of chaotic drug use, frequently reverting to street drugs. When she was using street drugs she was also a sex worker, to pay for the drugs. Louise had a 14-year-old daughter, Dolly, and a six-week-old baby, Belle. She had been stable on methadone for 18 months, but there were many concerns about whether Louise would be able to maintain this, and the likely impact on her baby. Previously she had always brought her clients back to her flat, and also dealt drugs there. Dolly lived with her grandmother but would visit her mother and Belle regularly. It had been agreed that Belle could remain with her mother, under close supervision. Belle was subject to a child protection plan. The plan was clear that if Louise reverted to street drugs and started dealing and selling herself in her flat, the local authority would apply for a court order, to remove Belle from her care. No one doubted how much Louise loved Belle; the question was whether she could protect her and prioritise her needs. Louise saw Belle as her chance to put things right after what she perceived as her failings with Dolly because she had not been able to care for her. She was so anxious to succeed, she was putting a lot of pressure on herself, plus she had the additional pressure of all the professionals she had to work with, their concerns, and the knowledge that if she went back to street drugs, the chances were she would lose Belle too.

One day I got a telephone call from Dolly, with whom I had a good relationship. She was in tears and asked me to meet her. I met her and we sat in the car, in a car park. She was very upset and I knew she would not want to be in a public space. Dolly told me that two weekends previously Louise had had a party.

Dolly had gone round when her mum was not expecting her, and the flat was full of people Dolly knew were using and dealing street drugs. There was drugs paraphernalia in the flat, and her mum was in the bedroom having sex with a man Dolly had never seen before. Dolly said she was 'off her head'. Belle was crying, her nappy was sodden, and she was starving. Dolly looked after Belle and took her back to their grandmother's. She did not tell her grandmother what she had found.

The next day Louise was full of remorse. She begged Dolly not to tell anyone what had happened at the weekend, and promised it would not happen again. She had got the flat cleaned up, and when Dolly took Belle back, everything looked better. Nothing else had happened since, as far as Dolly knew.

Dolly was desperately torn. She loved her mother and knew it would break her heart if Belle was taken away from her, but she also loved Belle and knew how fragile she was. She also knew that if Belle was taken away from her mother, there was a strong chance Louise would start using street drugs again and put herself in danger. She did not know what to do. Dolly had wrestled with this for two weeks. Because of her age and her level of maturity, she fully understood what the likely consequences would be if she told her grandmother, or professionals, about this.

Luckily she and I had built up a good relationship and she decided she had to tell me. Children of this age often find themselves in these impossible positions, usually when they have younger siblings they want to protect. It is easy to overlook what impact that would have on a child, having to make a decision like that, and if a child is brave enough to tell you what is happening, make sure you acknowledge how hard it must have been for her, and how brave she is for doing it. That child also needs to know how she has improved another child's life because of her braveness.

How to build a relationship with the child

Be aware of the huge power imbalance there will be in your relationship with the child. Not only in the adult/child relationship, but also the fact that you are the social worker, and in that child's eyes you have the power to take him, or his siblings, away from his parents, if he is still living at home, or to move him from somewhere he wants to live.

Children living in traumatic circumstances will very often build barriers to protect themselves. So on the outside, they are hard, cold and intimidating, but in the words of Camila Batmanghelidjh, founder of Kids Company, a charity that works with some of our most vulnerable children who are struggling to survive brutal childhoods and who often turn to gangs to be their 'family', 'I'd meet guys who were terrorising the whole of South London, but when I sat down and talked to them, I'd find that they were having night terrors and wetting the bed.'[4] So just remember that, for all the bravado, if you can call it that, on the outside, inside these are frightened children who have had to become this way to survive.

REMEMBER...

As always, when working with parents who are vulnerable, bear in mind how much you tell their children and how you do it. You can only make that decision on a case-by-case basis, however.

For example, a mother suffers from a mental illness that can be managed effectively if she takes her medication, but she does not want to take it because of the side effects, and you know the risks if she does not take her medication. Historically she has had episodes where she has left her home naked and has had sex with strangers in the street at 3am. She has run through traffic, laughing hysterically and pulling her clothes off, and done many other things she is deeply ashamed of when she is well.

Over the years she has generally been fine because she has taken her medication and has been perfectly able to care for her children, with support, from time to time. At this time, however, her mental health is deteriorating, her medication has become stronger, and so have the side

---

4   Quoted in O'Brien, C. (2012) 'The emotional casualty unit: A visit to Heart Yard, which offers sanctuary to troubled children.' Mail Online. 9 September. Available at www.dailymail.co.uk/home/you/article-2198765/A-visit-Heart-Yard-offers-sanctuary-troubled-children.html#ixzz2BvNZgVyJ

effects, and so she is reluctant to take her medication. Mental health professionals are concerned about the consequences and have made a referral to social care. There is a child protection conference and the oldest child, who is 15, is very supportive of his mother and helps with the care of the younger children; he wants to be at the conference, but how much should he be told?

You have to weigh up the mother's right to privacy along with her mortification about her behaviour when she is very unwell, with the need for this 15-year-old, who is a protective factor, not only for his younger siblings when their mother is unwell, but also for his mother, to know what the concerns are. The reports that are for the child protection conference should be general about her being unable to keep herself safe when she is very unwell, but don't go into the specifics of what she does. It is enough for the child to know that, and to know what he should do in those circumstances. You could have a bit at the beginning of the conference where you say to the child that because of confidentiality you will just have 15 minutes to discuss some aspects of the case. The professionals could then share and discuss those concerns with the mother, but then, when her son comes in, the conversation becomes general again.

Last, but not least, be respectful. Too often we hear young people saying that social workers are always late, or they do not turn up when they say they will, or they take calls during their appointment. Put yourself on the receiving end of that. We all know how infuriating it is if someone is always late – it is just like saying that they are not prioritising your time together. There are some times when it is unavoidable, but this should be the exception and not the rule, and you should always let them know if this is the case. Don't take calls when you are with a young person, except if it is an absolute emergency, and then explain first that a call might come through that you will have to take. Again, we all know what it feels like when we are with someone, whether it is a friend, or another professional, who chats away on their mobile while we stare into space. It is very disrespectful and will give the child the message that they are not as important as the person to whom you are speaking. Treating young people in this way will damage your relationship considerably.

Think also about the practicalities – you want the child to ring you if she is worried about anything, but what about the cost of the call? She could always text you, and you could ring her back. Give her a direct line, or your work mobile, so she is not left waiting for ages, which costs her money and wastes her time. Children will soon give up contacting you if you make it difficult to do so.

This is the age range where you have to be particularly careful about not sharing too much information about yourself. Professionals may genuinely believe that by telling the young person they understand because they were sexually abused too, may help them, but it is our empathy the child needs, not our own experiences.

Where best to see the child

Again, this has to be made on a case-by-case basis, but think about what would be right for that child. For most children we are working with at this age, the reason we are working with them is either because of concerns about what is happening in the home, or because they are beyond parental control. In many cases the home will not be a safe place, and therefore not the best place to see them. For other children, however, the home is their safe place and they do not want to leave it.

Case example: Where to see a child

Vicky had been a victim of child sexual exploitation. She did not come from an abusive home, but had got mixed up with girls at school who were mixing with young male adults, and she was impressed. As can be the case with child sexual exploitation, the girls did not see that they were being groomed, and when it reached the point of sexual abuse, Vicky was in too deep. She did not feel able to tell her parents because her 'boyfriend' had told her they would not believe her anyway, and they would think she was disgusting for sleeping around.

So she was trapped. Vicky was in this cycle for several months before she felt able to tell someone what was happening. Social care became involved and Vicky did not want to leave the home because she had become so fearful. In that situation it was absolutely right to see Vicky in the home, until she felt able to leave it.

Ask the child where they would like to meet, suggest places if they are not sure, although some environments are definitely more conducive to private conversations than others – I worked in an office once where another department's desks were just by our interview rooms. Once or twice I would have someone in floods of tears, talking about something terrible that had happened, and I would hear roars of laughter from the team outside. It was extremely unhelpful that the interview rooms were so close to this department, because they were not social workers and did not understand how sensitive our conversations can be.

Everything I have written so far addresses the child who is willing to engage with you, but what do you do with the one who refuses to, because there will, of course, be those children?

Case example: How to engage with hard to reach children

I was doing my first home visit to a family where there was domestic abuse. In this case the mother was the perpetrator and the father was the victim. The boy, Sam, was 13. He was struggling to understand why his father did not just hit his mother back, and he said he thought his father was 'a wimp'. Sam had started to become really angry and was becoming physically abusive towards his father. There were also concerns that his mother was being physically abusive towards Sam. His attendance at school had dropped right off, and I knew that Sam was terrified the children at school would find out what was happening at home and he would be the laughing stock.

Initially I spoke to the parents; Sam was up in his bedroom. The mother acknowledged she had got a problem, but said she was only violent when she had had a drink, so she was trying to cut down. I spent some time with the parents, and then asked to see Sam. The father called Sam down, but he refused to come down to see me.

Sam's father went up to try to persuade him to come down, but he still refused. I then asked the parents if they would mind if I went upstairs. They pointed me in the direction of Sam's bedroom.

I knocked on the bedroom door.

> Me: 'Hello Sam, my name is Joanna. I know Dad has told you I am a social worker and I have come to see mum and dad and you. Would it be okay if I came in and talked to you?'

> Sam: 'F*** off.'

> Me: 'The thing is, Sam, I am going to be coming round for a while and trying to help sort out what is going on at home, and to try and help make things better for you, but what I really don't want is for everyone to make lots of decisions but you not to be part of that. You are old enough to be told about what is going on and to be part of any decisions that are made, but we can only do that if you will talk to me.'

Silence.

> Me: 'I'll tell you what, Sam. What about if I come in for five minutes, just so I can explain what is going to happen next. I have to go soon and I don't want to leave without talking to you, telling you what's happening and hearing what you think about everything, but I can't talk about those things through a door. Can I come in for five minutes and then I will leave you in peace?'

Sam flings open the door and stomps back to his bed, where he sits with his back to me.

> Me: 'Thank you, Sam.'

I kept to my word, and stood just inside the door and explained why I was there. I then said I would be back next week and I was leaving my number on his desk so he could text me if he wanted to.

The point is, that for all Sam's reluctance, he opened the door, literally and metaphorically, and now it was up to me to try to show Sam that I was not a threat.

If children continue to refuse to see their social worker, it is something that managers should keep an eye on, in case it is a pattern of behaviour with a particular social worker. Don't always assume that the child is the one with the 'problem'.

Communicating with a child with a learning disability

The most important thing is to be prepared. Many social workers who work in child protection are not working with children with disabilities all the time, and therefore they cannot be expected to be experts in communication with children with disabilities. The reassuring part is that there will always be someone who is. So before you do your first visit, find out whether the child has any communication difficulties or not, and if they do, seek advice. Speak to the teacher and ask for their advice. Always ask parents too, of course, but sometimes you can get a different response from parents and professionals.

Case example: Using others' expertise

I was involved in a child protection investigation. There were concerns of neglect, and I knew the child, Tom, who was five, had a learning disability. I did not know the level of disability, but it was the school that had made the referral, so before I visited the child at home, I telephoned the school and spoke to the teacher, who had made the referral. Along with the other questions we ask, I asked her about communication – would Tom understand me? Did he have any communication difficulties? The teacher said that he would understand me, as long as I kept my language very simple, but that I might not understand his responses. She suggested that I see Tom at school, where she could join me, and then she could explain what Tom was saying.

I visited the mother at home and talked through the concerns. I then explained that I would need to see Tom and that I would like to see him at school, to see how he was in that environment, and his teacher would be able to help if I could not understand what Tom was saying. (I wanted to see Tom at school first, where the teacher could help with communication, and also in an environment where it seemed he was happy and not anxious. When I then saw him at home I would be able to see if his behaviour was different in each place.)

Too often we see the disability and not the child. Even if children are non-verbal, there may well be ways they can communicate. A parent or a worker who is attuned to that child will know, just as parents know what it is their baby needs. Parents understand what a particular cry means. In some cases it will be the worker who knows the child better than the primary carer, however, and this is why it is essential that we work closely with the other professionals, as well as with the parents.

3 Disguised Compliance, Non-Compliance and Hostility

Disguised compliance

The term 'disguised compliance' has been attributed to Peter Reder, Sylvia Duncan and Moira Gray, who outlined this type of behaviour in their book, *Beyond Blame: Child Abuse Tragedies Revisited.*[1] The NSPCC defines it as involving 'a parent or carer giving the appearance of co-operating with child welfare agencies to avoid raising suspicions, to allay professional concerns and ultimately to diffuse professional intervention.'[2]

Before I write anything else about disguised compliance, I would like you to consider this – a room full of people who are standing up. They are asked to sit down if they have ever tidied their home before a professional comes round. Then those still standing are asked to sit down if they have ever tidied their home before their mum comes round. Then the very few who are still standing are asked to sit down if they have ever been economical with the truth with their doctor about how much they weigh, smoke or drink. How many do you think are still standing at this point? I wonder if you would be? I certainly would not – I would have fallen at the

1   Reder, P., Duncan, S. and Gray, M. (1993) *Beyond Blame: Child Abuse Tragedies Revisited.* London: Routledge.
2   NSPCC (2010) Disguised Compliance – An NSPCC Factsheet. Available at www.nspcc.org.uk/globalassets/documents/information-service/factsheet-disguised-compliance1.pdf

first hurdle, and the second and the third. My point is that, just as with other professionals, this is not a 'them and us' situation. Disguised compliance is often described as a bad thing that these terrible parents do, but it is the most natural thing in the world. Most parents do not want their child taken away from them. Most parents we work with love their children, even if they are not able to prioritise their children's needs. It might make our job a lot harder, and it can certainly impact negatively on children, but it is not necessarily a 'bad' thing; it depends entirely on the motive.

Case example: Reasons for disguised compliance

I went to interview a mother as part of a serious case review. She had been in an abusive relationship with a partner she was not supposed to be in contact with. There were lots of other issues as well, and her children had been the subject of child protection plans at the time of one child's death.

When I talked to the mother about how life had been when her child was still alive and all these professionals had been working with her and her family, she told me it had been impossible. She said she would tell the social worker she was doing everything the child protection plan asked of her because, in her mind, if she did not say that, her children would be taken away from her, and realistically, they may well have been. She liked her social worker, but she said to me, 'I did not know who to be more frightened of, my ex-partner or the social worker.'

Having said that, there will, of course, be cases where disguised compliance is used in a more sinister way by perpetrators who want to divert our attention away from the truth. I recently had sight of a letter from a father, a convicted sex offender, who had been sexually abusing his own children, that had been sent to the local authority. In the letter the father explained how easy it had been to divert social care's attention away from him by telling them of worrying behaviour by other people. His motive was entirely sinister, and the letter, chilling.

So what we have to do is work out if the family is using disguised compliance as a tactic to placate us, and remember that this may not always be being done consciously. How can we tell? This is often where gut instinct comes in. You just know, you have a feeling, but you cannot prove it.

Case example: Gut instinct

I was working with a mother who had three young children. The father of the first two had disappeared, but the father of the third little boy was around. He was a convicted sex offender and was considered to be at a high risk of re-offending. The children he had sexually abused before had been young boys, of a similar age to the two older boys. We only knew of his history accidentally, because he changed his name on a fairly regular basis.

The children were all placed on child protection plans, and the mother agreed that she would not let the father have contact with any of the children. She also told us she had ended the relationship when she had found out about his history. The trouble was, I did not believe her. I had absolutely no proof, but I was convinced they were still together and that he was spending time with her, but without evidence, we had no grounds to go to court requesting that the children be removed from her care.

Luckily I had built up a good relationship with the people around the mother, and one day, one of them telephoned me and told me the couple had got married. Once I could prove this, it gave me the evidence we needed to go to court.

The most important thing is always the outcome for the child, and in this case, a family member on the mother's side agreed to have all three boys, and the mother was able to spend as much time with them as she wanted, but they were always supervised by a protective family member.

In Chapter 1 we looked at neglect and the impact of neglect. We commonly see disguised compliance in neglect cases, and the evidence is easier to find than you may think.

We spend a lot of time discussing whether a parent has the capacity to change. What we really mean by that is, do they have the mental capacity, or do they have a learning difficulty? What we often forget, or do not know, is that there are two components to capacity. The first is motivation, and the second is mental capacity. If either of these is missing, the parent may be unable to change.

Case example: Motivation to change

A mother came to the attention of social care. She had recently moved to the UK from Africa, and there was a concern that she was not bonding with her children. A parenting assessment was done and the conclusion was that there seemed to be 'very poor attachment' and there were grave concerns about her children.

Workers kept telling the mother she needed to play with her children and talk to them, and she kept saying she was and she would, but she never did.

Eventually the workers established that in the woman's tribe in Africa the mothers had very little to do with the children because they were too busy collecting water and firewood and cooking, cleaning and washing. It was the elder women of the tribe who cared for the children, and in their culture adults did not play with children as we, in our culture, expect. The trouble was that this mother was now living in a flat in a city, she was very isolated, and knew very few people, and so both she and the children were very alone.

Once the workers realised this, they could help in a much more constructive way. Just telling the mother what we in the West expect of parents is fruitless.

Be very mindful of this when you are working with a family from the black and minority ethnic (BME) community, as they may have a very different culture. The most effective way to work with any family is by asking rather than telling. Ask questions about their culture, and this is as true of the white, British family as it is of the family that has just arrived from Afghanistan. Do not assume because a family is white British that they will have the same culture and values as you.

REMEMBER...

There are two components to the capacity to change – one is the mental capacity to do it, the other, the motivation.

There are many families who do not see the value of an education. Just telling someone their child has to go to school will get you nowhere. Our starting point should be to try to understand why education is not important to the family, listening before you speak.

When we are thinking about whether a parent has the capacity to change, we often focus on whether we can fund an assessment. Assessments are expensive and are usually not done until we get into the arena of legal proceedings. Very often the evidence is there, but we have missed it.

So how can we tell? In Chapter 7 we will look at using multi-agency chronologies because they show us patterns of behaviour, as well as what else is happening for the family, and how effectively we are working with the family. Even if your local authority does not use them routinely, if you have a complex neglect case you are all grappling with, compile a multi-agency chronology because it will give you insight.

In *Working Together to Safeguard Children, 2013*, it says,

> The assessment of neglect cases can be difficult. Neglect can fluctuate both in level and duration. A child's welfare can, for example, improve following input from services or a change in circumstances and review, but then deteriorate once support is removed. Professionals should be wary of being too optimistic. Timely and decisive action is critical to ensure that children are not left in neglectful homes.[3] (p.24)

With some families you will notice that things get better when an agency mentions social care, or when there is talk of a child protection plan, but then things deteriorate when the child is no longer on the plan, or social care closes the case. What that demonstrates very clearly is that the family has the mental capacity to make the changes deemed necessary, but the motivation has been to get social care off their backs. It is showing you that those areas of improvement you have identified, whatever the parents have said,

---

3   Department for Education (2013) Working Together to Safeguard Children: A Guide to Interagency Working to Safeguard and Promote the Welfare of Children. London: Department for Education.

they do not think are important. What is important to these parents is getting rid of social care.

Sometimes improvements are only made with professional support for very understandable reasons, the family were really struggling and did not know what to do. They really needed the extra support and, with the right support, they were able to make the changes required.

Disguised compliance and domestic abuse

Disguised compliance is a common factor in domestic abuse cases because, as we saw in the first case example in this chapter, the mother is caught between the perpetrator and the authorities. The perpetrator is controlling her, and the authorities are trying to control what she does.

Our understanding of domestic abuse is increasing all the time, but there are many professionals who underestimate the force of domestic abuse. It can never be as simple as telling a mother she must not see X, or that she must not let X have contact with the children. The mother will tell us she will not, but when we leave, who is there to protect her? She cannot control what the perpetrator does, but she cannot tell us that because if she does, she is frightened that we will take her children away.

We consider domestic abuse in greater detail in Chapter 4, but at this stage, remember that disguised compliance is very common in cases of domestic abuse, for very understandable reasons.

Risk factors of disguised compliance

There are a number of risks to children if disguised compliance is an element of the dynamics within the family/professional relationship. The most important is that professionals will not have a clear picture of what is actually going on, they will not be able to assess levels of risk, and therefore concerns can be downgraded. It is these cases that can be left to drift because no one really knows what is going on. The mother keeps telling you everything is fine and seems to be working really well with you, but what you keep having to go back to is, *what is the evidence of change?* In the words of Brandon *et al.* (2008), 'Apparent or disguised cooperation from parents often prevented or delayed understanding of the severity of harm to the child and cases drifted. Where parents...engineered the focus away from allegations of harm, children went unseen and unheard.'[4]

A common feature of serious case reviews is that we have not kept the child at the centre of what we are doing. Disguised compliance can lead to a focus on adults and their engagement with services, but also, in most child protection cases, the adults we are working with will have very real needs of their own. We examine this in greater detail in Chapter 4, but we know that domestic abuse, mental ill health and/or substance misuse was a factor in 86 per cent of all serious case reviews carried out between 2009–11.[5] We cannot overlook the needs of the parents, as their needs will be interwoven with the needs of their child. The trouble is, that this can detract away from the child, and can end up with us focusing almost entirely on the needs of the adult.

Case example: Victoria Climbié[6]

On one occasion the social worker did a home visit. In her recording she wrote a whole page on the great aunt's housing needs, and Victoria was only mentioned in one line at the bottom. The recording

---

4   Brandon, M., Belderson, P., Warren, C., Howe, D., Gardner, R., Dodsworth, J. and Black, J. (2008) Analysing Child Deaths and Serious Injury through Abuse and Neglect: What can we learn? A biennial analysis of serious case reviews 2003-2005. London: Department for Education and Skills. Available at   http://webarchive.nationalarchives.gov.uk/20130401151715/https://www.education.gov.uk/publications/eorderingdownload/dcsf-rr023.pdf

5   Brandon, M., Sidebotham, P., Bailey, S., Belderson, P., Hawley, C., Ellis, C. and Megson, M. (2012) *New Learning from Serious Case Reviews: A Two Year Report for 2009–11.* London: Department for Education. Available at www.gov.uk/government/uploads/system/uploads/attachment_data/file/184053/DFE-RR226_Report.pdf

6   Laming, Lord (2003) *The Victoria Climbié Inquiry, Report of an Inquiry by Lord Laming.* London: The Stationery Office. Available at www.gov.uk/government/uploads/system/uploads/attachment_data/file/273183/5730.pdf

said that Victoria was well dressed, sitting on the floor, and playing with a doll.

We now know that that was the time that Victoria was being kept in the bath. She was tied up and kept in a bin bag, lying in her own excrement and urine. She actually died from hypothermia because the bathroom was freezing cold.

Presumably the reason why Victoria was sitting on the floor throughout the visit was because she could not stand up straight as a result of being tied up most of the time – her body had become bent. The great aunt's partner, Carl Manning, also said that there was a box of dolls and toys in the flat, but Victoria was not allowed to play with them. They were only there for when the professionals visited.

It is not uncommon to read in serious case reviews that the parents have controlled the visits made by professionals and the professionals' contact with the children.

Another general risk factor, which can also be relevant in disguised compliance cases, is that we can be over-optimistic about progress being achieved. We want things to get better for the child, we want to believe that parents want the best for their children and will protect them from maltreatment, so we latch on to the simple things we can measure – the state of the home, attending appointments, going to groups. We look at this in greater detail later, in Chapter 7, but for now, remember that it can be disguised compliance that is leading us to have false hope.

What does disguised compliance look like?

Disguised compliance can take a number of different forms. Sometimes a parent will say to you, 'You are the only one who understands me. You are the only one who really helps.' Sometimes that is meant sincerely and is heart-felt and it can make you feel good – after all, it is important that we build a rapport with the families we work with. But bear in mind that sometimes this is used as a tactic to alienate other professionals, and some parents use this very effectively.

Case example: Seduced by parents

I worked with a mother who used to say to professionals, 'You are the only one who really helps me and understands me', but what she would do was move around the professionals when she thought her current 'favourite' was no longer on her side.

We all felt flattered and were seduced by this until we realised that she was doing it to everyone, one by one.

Sometimes parents will engage well with one set of professionals, for example, health professionals, to deflect attention from their lack of engagement with other services. Parents may also criticise other professionals to divert attention away from their own behaviour. (A very effective way of doing this is when a parent goes to the local MP. There is usually an uproar, and the focus is diverted entirely away from the child, to the professionals' practice.)

We look at unannounced home visits in Chapter 5, but it is important to consider here, in the context of disguised compliance, that some families will clean up just for our visit and make sure anyone who is not supposed to be there is out of the way, if they know professionals are coming round.

Some parents will agree to do whatever is asked of them at a child protection conference, but then they do nothing, or they do just enough to keep the professionals happy. The parents may start to avoid the professionals, so they do not have to face them. Or they meet and there is a string of reasons why they have not been able to do what has been asked of them, but they have managed to do other things.

REMEMBER...

There are some families who have been involved with social care for so long, they know how the system works, and they know what we want to hear and what we put value on.

Always make sure you are informed by evidence of change, rather than what you are being told.

In Chapter 7 we examine how we can work more constructively and effectively with families generally, but there are some factors that are particularly relevant when dealing with disguised compliance, and so I set them out here as well:

> Decisions must be based on evidence and facts, not what you are being told by parents, whether that be in terms of excuses, reassurances or assertions that they are just about to start doing what you said was so important.

> Use the evidence and the facts to establish what changes have actually been made, and how they have improved the child's life, or left the child at greater risk.

There is always a balance between giving the parents enough time to make and sustain the changes required, and not allowing further damage to a child. As discussed in Chapter 1 on neglect, we know that for too long we have left children languishing in homes, living with chronic neglect. We must not respond to that by leaping in and trying to remove children from their parents without giving the parent the opportunity to make the changes, unless, of course, we have grave concerns about the immediate protection of the child. There is a balance, and this decision can only be made on a case-by-case basis.

Non-compliance and hostility

Working with non-compliance is very different from working with disguised compliance. At least you know where you stand with the family that tells you to 'F*** off'.

The first thing to do is try to understand why the family will not work with you. Very often it is the fear of having their children taken away, and it is up to all of us to explain to families that only a tiny percentage of children are actually taken into care.

Myth: 'All social workers do is take children away'

Here is the reality as at October 2014:[7]

› 11 million children in the UK

› 657,800 referrals to social care

› 441,500 initial assessments

› 397,600 children in need

› 48,300 children subject to child protection plans.

There were 68,840 children in care in March 2014.[8]

The challenge is, of course, that we can never say 'We will not take your children away', but as you can see from the statistics, and you will know yourselves, much of the work we do in child protection is try to keep families together.

The nature of the work we do in child protection means that at times there will be families who feel angry and hostile towards us, and again, this is very natural. Some, however, behave in a threatening way, which can be very frightening. We know from frontline social workers, health visitors and police officers that verbal abuse and threats of violence are common. Abuse comes with the territory because of the fear we are going to take their children away; this is not to excuse abuse, but we do have to accept that it is part of our job and learn how best to deal with it, while keeping ourselves and our colleagues as safe as possible. (I will come to the children later.)

We do not always know when a situation is going to become hostile, and so we always need to be aware. We do know that many of the parents we work with will be perpetrators or victims of domestic

---

7   Department for Education (2014) 'Characteristics of Children in Need in England, 2013–14' Statistical First Release. Available at www.gov.uk/government/uploads/system/uploads/attachment_data/file/367877/SFR43_2014_Main_Text.pdf

8   Department for Education (2014) Children Looked After in England (Including Adoption and Care Leavers) Year Ending March 2014. London: Department for Education. Available at www.gov.uk/government/uploads/system/uploads/attachment_data/file/359277/SFR36_2014_Text.pdf

abuse, many will be misusing substances, and many will be suffering from undiagnosed or untreated mental illnesses. Of course none of those factors mean that the person will automatically be violent, but these issues may well exacerbate an already sensitive situation.

It is not just up to us as individuals to keep ourselves safe. Our employers have responsibilities too, under the Health and Safety at Work Act 1974, the management of Health and Safety at Work Regulations and the Workplace Regulations 1992.

In order to keep yourself as safe as possible, find out as much as you can about a family before you visit them, or before they come to the office. If you are visiting the family home, make sure you go with someone else if you are concerned. We are less physically vulnerable if there are two of us, and it is usually the case that people are less likely to be threatening, or intimidating, or violent if there is a witness (I write about this in greater detail in Chapter 5). Make sure you meet the family in a room where you can make a quick exit if you need to, and if you are in the home, sit near the door. Wear clothes you can run in, if need be. If you feel the tension rising, you can always say you just have to step out for a minute to get something from the car, or something from your office.

Always make sure you have a plan. Think about what you would do if the service user did become aggressive, and if there are two of you, think about whether one of you deals with the issues that brought you there and the other deals with any hostile behaviour. Play to your strengths.

Make sure you have an exit strategy if the situation becomes too dangerous. I would always try to be honest and address any threatening behaviour straight away. Just be straightforward and say something like, 'I can see you are angry and we are not going to get anywhere while you are so cross, so we can't carry on with this meeting while you are so cross. It is also not okay for you to shout at me. So I am going to end this meeting now and I will ring you later, when you have had a chance to calm down, and we can then talk about what is going to happen next.'

When you leave you will probably feel a bit shaky. That is fine. It is completely normal to feel scared if someone is threatening and frightening.

Don't bottle it up – that is how people burn out. Talk to your manager, talk to your team. The best and most productive teams are the ones where the workers support each other. I have worked in some fantastic teams over the years, and that is what keeps you going in such situations.

For all that I have said about working with non-compliance and hostility, ask yourself one question – why it is okay for a child to be living in a home that you and other professionals are too afraid, for very good reasons, to visit? I have known families over the years where uniformed police officers visit with the social worker because of the situation. There are children living in those homes too. How can they possibly be safe if adults are not?

Disguised and non-compliance in serious case reviews

There are many examples of disguised compliance in serious case reviews, some of which I have mentioned already.

In the most recent high profile serious case reviews, there was only a single mention of disguised compliance in Daniel Pelka's serious case review,[9] and this was regarding education. One of the concerns was around Daniel and his siblings' attendance at school. Every so often this improved, but then it dipped again.

In the Hamza Khan serious case review, there was no mention of disguised compliance, but the mother was known to be non-compliant with most of the agencies. The mother's 'antagonism to hospitals and health staff was generally known about from early on and was used to rationalise the absence of contact with the primary health services. It had implications for late ante natal care, post natal support and the on-going care and immunisations of the children.'[10]

---

9 Lock, R. (2013) *Serious Case Review Re Daniel Pelka*. Coventry Safeguarding Children Board. Available at www.coventrylscb.org.uk/files/SCR/FINAL%20 Overview%20Report%20%20DP%2013090913%20Publication%20version. pdf

10 Bradford Safeguarding Children Board (2013) *A Serious Case Review. Hamzah Khan. The Overview Report.* Available at www.bradford-scb.org. uk/scr/hamzah_khan_scr/Serious%20Case%20Reveiw%20Overview%20 Report%20November%202013.pdf

On one occasion a nursery nurse attempted a home visit but was rebuffed by a hostile Amanda Hutton, the mother, and an older sibling. The nursery nurse saw a child who looked pale and told the health visitor, but nothing more was done.

In the case of Khyra Ishaq, the little girl who died in Birmingham, the mother, Angela Gordon, was so aggressive that the teacher and social workers feared for their physical safety. Angela Gordon made allegations of racism and complaints of harassment. In the words of the serious case review,

> Adult resistance to professional intervention, doorstep conversations, the mother's sound knowledge of home education legislation and a hostile and aggressive approach, influenced and affected professional actions, preventing a full understanding of conditions within the home and seemed to render professionals impotent, thereby directing the focus away from the welfare of the children. Adults within the household fully controlled, monitored and limited access to the children and through their behaviours and attitudes frustrated a thorough analysis and assessment of the issues. The approach reinforced that the power dynamics lay with the parents and not with the rights, welfare and protection of the children.

The review went on to say:

> The complaint raised by the mother in February 2008, within the Children's Social Care complaints process, following the initial assessment visit above, appeared to impact upon the Children's Social Care manager and practitioner. This action appears to have generated a reluctance to follow through on plans with a partner agency to effectively pursue assessment processes, for fear of wider repercussions within the complaints process.

Angela Gordon had complained about racism. We look at that in greater detail later, in Chapter 6, where we consider further areas of complexities for professionals. On one occasion the education social worker attempted a home visit, 'but was prevented from access to the house by the mother who was hostile and quoting her human rights'. This happened on more than one occasion.

(This serious case review is no longer available online.)

There are differing views of disguised compliance being evident in the case of Peter Connelly. According to the first serious case review:

> It appears that many of the features of disguised compliance did not exist in this case (recognisable ambivalence, avoidance, confrontation or violence) or did not present in the ways described by Brandon et al and by Reder & Duncan. The extent to which the concept of 'disguised' or 'apparent' compliance is relevant to Ms A's [the mother's] behaviour therefore remains unproven, though the criminal proceedings may shed more light on the relevance of it.[11]

The second serious case review makes no mention of disguised compliance.

There is another area in which we see disguised, or non-compliance, being used very effectively to stymie professional intervention, and that is class, or socioeconomic status. We look at this in greater detail in the section, Socioeconomic groups, in Chapter 6, but I want to highlight here a serious case review that took place in East Cheshire. This was a case where three siblings had been abused for over ten years. They had been adopted by a couple who put down 'child B's' behaviour to his start in life. The serious case review found that:

> ...the abuse was both predictable and preventable. Too many professionals misread the signals and thought Child B was running away as part of normal teenage rebellion against the parents' discipline. They were lulled by the parents' disguised compliance. The parents presented as being concerned for

---

11   Department for Education (2010) *Haringey Local Safeguarding Children Board. Serious Case Review. 'Child A.'* November 2008. Available at www.gov. uk/government/uploads/system/uploads/attachment_data/file/182527/first_ serious_case_review_overview_report_relating_to_peter_connelly_dated_ november_2008.pdf

Child B's welfare – which to an extent they may have been. They usually reported him missing, and often made efforts themselves to locate him. In addition they were active in supporting the High School's efforts to deal with his challenging behaviour and running away from school.

The review went on to say,

> In this case, many professionals struggled to maintain a child focus when faced with the parents' aggressive behaviour and their 'disguised compliance' and the professionals' approach was affected by perceptions and assumptions made regarding the parents' social class, professional status (scientists), and high academic qualifications, and the attitude of the parents towards them.[12]

I hope what you take from this chapter is that we have to strip away what we are being told, strip away race, culture, ethnicity, class and socioeconomic status, and focus on the evidence. Every child in this country deserves the same level of protection, and we must get better at not being diverted by all the other factors.

---

12 Cheshire East Safeguarding Children's Board (2001) Serious Case Review CE001. Child B, Child C, Child D. Executive Summary. Available at www. cheshireeastlscb.org.uk/pdf/scr-executive-summary.pdf

4 Multiple Risk Factors

As set out in the other chapters, none of the risk factors described in this chapter are predictors of child abuse, but together, domestic abuse, substance misuse and mental ill health are sometimes referred to as the 'toxic trio' because they have been identified as common features of families where domestic abuse and child abuse have occurred. We use them as possible indicators of increased risk of harm to children and young people because they can adversely affect a parent's ability to be a good parent. However, it is important to remember that some children living with one or more of these adverse factors will not come to any harm, depending on the other variants in their lives. Every situation is unique, and every child is unique.

REMEMBER...

Every child is unique and there are no givens.

At the end of the communist regime I went to work in an orphanage in Romania for three months. Out of the 500 children in the orphanage, about 480 lay in metal cots all day, rocking and banging their heads, or locked in rooms. The other 20 could walk and talk, and some were used to taking laundry, food etc. around the orphanage. Their quality of life was a million times better than the children who lay in cots, locked in rooms all day – but it is all relative. I used to look at the few who were allowed out of their rooms, and wonder what they had that meant they had learnt to walk and talk, and whatever their level of learning difficulty was, it was a difficulty, not a disability.

The point is, that there are always exceptions, and we can never say that a child who grows up living with these adversities will definitely be a certain way.

Some facts and figures

Between 2009 and 2011, domestic abuse, substance misuse and/or mental ill health were factors in 86 per cent of all serious case reviews during that period. Although the data is currently not drawn together, we see this same high level reflected in serious case reviews throughout the later years too.

In a study of 338 cases across different local authorities, domestic violence featured in 60 per cent of the referrals, parental substance misuse in just over half (52 per cent) of cases, and both issues were present in a fifth (20 per cent) of cases.[1]

Domestic abuse

Language

Why do some people talk about 'domestic abuse' and others 'domestic violence'?

The two terms are interchangeable. It always used to be referred to as domestic violence, but as more was understood about the elements of the abuse that were not physically violent, the control, the coercion, some felt the term 'domestic abuse' should be used instead.

Some facts and figures

> Two women die every week at the hands of their current or former partner. On average, a woman will experience 35 assaults before going to the police.

---

1   Cleaver, H., Nicholson, D., Tarr, S. and Cleaver, D. (2007) *Child Protection, Domestic Violence and Parental Substance Misuse: Family Experiences and Effective Practice*. London: Jessica Kingsley Publishers.

> › Domestic abuse often starts or intensifies during and after pregnancy.

> › Disabled women are twice as likely to experience domestic violence and abuse as non-disabled women, and over a longer period of time, suffering more severe injuries as a result of the violence.

> › Domestic violence and abuse in teen relationships is increasingly recognised as a serious issue. Research now suggests that women between the ages of 16 and 25 are at highest risk.[2]

> › Seventy per cent of victims at high risk of serious harm have children, the majority of whom are under five years old.[3]

> › In the most recent Crime Survey for England and Wales domestic violence accounts for 21 per cent of all recorded violent crime.[4]

> › In nearly two thirds of serious case reviews between 2009–11, domestic abuse was a factor.[5]

> › As set out in the Introduction to this book, women can be perpetrators and men can be victims, and domestic abuse

2   Health Visiting and School Nursing Programmes: Supporting Implementation of the New Service Model. Leaflet No. 5: Domestic Violence and Abuse – Professional Guidance. Department of Health. Available at www.gov.uk/government/uploads/system/uploads/attachment_data/file/211018/9576-TSO-Health_Visiting_Domestic_Violence_A3_Posters_WEB.pdf

3   SafeLives (no date) Available at www.caada.org.uk/policy/Safety_in_Numbers_full_report.pdf

4   Office for National Statistics (2015) Available at www.ons.gov.uk/ons/rel/crime-stats/crime-statistics/focus-on-violent-crime-and-sexual-offences--2013-14/rpt-chapter-1.html?format=print

5   Brandon, M., Sidebotham, P., Bailey, S., Belderson, P., Hawley, C., Ellis, C. and Megson, M. (2012) *New Learning from Serious Case Reviews: A Two Year Report for 2009–11*. London: Department for Education. Available at www.gov.uk/government/uploads/system/uploads/attachment_data/file/184053/DFE-RR226_Report.pdf

occurs in same-sex relationships too, but research has shown that 89 per cent of victims of four or more incidents of domestic abuse are women.[6] This is predominantly a male to female crime.

> Twenty years ago the police would not attend a domestic abuse incident in the home because it was seen to be a private incident between a man and a woman. There was only a concern about a child in the context of domestic abuse if they had received a physical injury.

> Ten years ago it was very unusual to have a child made the subject of a child protection plan because of emotional abuse, but now it is the second largest category, after neglect. Last year, 32 per cent of all children on a child protection plan in England were under the category of 'emotional abuse'.[7] The reason for this is because of the increased understanding of domestic abuse brought about by research, and the impact it has on children, even if the children are not being directly harmed themselves. In 2002 there was a change in legislation, and a child witnessing domestic abuse became recognised as 'significant harm' in the Adoption and Children Act 2002. The definition of 'harm' in England and Wales was amended to include 'impairment suffered from seeing or hearing the ill-treatment of another.' Witnessing domestic abuse is also recognised as harm in the Family Law (Scotland) Act 2006.

6   Walby, S. and Allen, J. (2004) *Domestic Violence, Sexual Assault and Stalking: Findings from the British Crime Survey.* March. London: Home Office Research, Development and Statistics Directorate. Available at www.avaproject.org.uk/media/28792/hors276.pdf

7   NSPCC (2014) Child Protection Register Statistics. England 2010-2014. Available at www.nspcc.org.uk/globalassets/documents/statistics-and-information/child-protection-register-statistics-england.pdf

Domestic abuse and research

In recent years, there has been a surge of research into early brain development, including in utero. New technologies, such as neuroimaging techniques, are providing us with increased insight into how the brain develops, and how early experiences affect that development. One area that has been receiving increasing research attention involves the effects of maltreatment generally on the developing brain, especially during infancy and early childhood. Much of this research is providing biological explanations for what practitioners have long been describing in psychological, emotional and behavioural terms, and there is now scientific evidence of altered brain functioning as a result of early maltreatment.

This emerging body of knowledge has many implications for the prevention and treatment of child maltreatment, and is informing and shaping policy and practice today.

There is a growing body of research that shows evidence of a negative impact on the baby's brain, both pre- and post-natal, when the baby is exposed to extreme stress, including domestic abuse.

When the mother is in fight or flight mode, prior to or during an episode of violence, her brain releases cortisol, which is a toxin. The cortisol travels through the umbilical cord to the foetus's brain, which then triggers a release of cortisol in the foetus's brain. So what is happening is every time the attack is imminent, the foetus is receiving a double dose of the poison, cortisol. As the brain develops, it follows certain neural pathways, and some research has shown that the cortisol blocks the pathways so the brain has to re-route. What happens is that the make-up of the baby's brain, by the time it is born, may be different to a baby where there has not been this very high level of stress.[8]

This is not a view that is universally accepted by all researchers, but it is currently the predominant view. What seems to be generally accepted is that the brain is in a constant state of neuroplasticity,

8   National Scientific Council on the Developing Child. (2005/2014). Excessive Stress Disrupts the Architecture of the Developing Brain: Working Paper 3. Updated Edition. Available at http://developingchild.harvard.edu/resources/reports_and_working_papers/working_papers/wp3/

which means that it is changing all the time. Therefore interventions can be affective at any time during someone's lifetime, although, as discussed in Chapter 1, the earlier we can intervene, the more likely there will be a positive outcome for the child.

Once the baby is born there will be many factors that affect the continuing development of the brain, including whether the baby remains in the same environment, if the baby moves from placement to placement, or whether the child has stability in the long term with carers who are able to prioritise the child's needs.

A growing body of literature shows that children who have been exposed to domestic abuse are more likely than their peers to experience a wide range of difficulties, which fall into three main categories:

› *Behavioural, social, and emotional problems:* children in families experiencing domestic abuse are more likely than other children to exhibit aggressive and anti-social behaviour, or to be depressed or anxious. Researchers have also found higher levels of anger, hostility, oppositional behaviour and disobedience; fear and withdrawal; poor peer, sibling and social relationships; and low self-esteem.

› *Cognitive and attitudinal problems:* children exposed to domestic abuse are more likely to experience difficulties in school and score lower on assessments of verbal, motor and cognitive skills. Other issues identified in the research are slower cognitive development, lack of conflict resolution skills, limited problem-solving skills, pro-violence attitudes and belief in rigid gender stereotypes and male privilege.

› *Long-term problems:* research indicates that males exposed to domestic violence as children are more likely to engage in domestic violence as adults; similarly, females are more likely to be victims. Higher levels of adult depression and trauma symptoms have also been found.

As always, it is important to remember that not all children exposed to domestic abuse will experience such negative effects.

Children's risk levels and reactions to domestic abuse exist on a continuum – some children demonstrate enormous resiliency, while others show signs of significant maladaptive adjustment. Protective factors such as social competence, intelligence, high self-esteem, outgoing temperament, strong sibling and peer relationships, and a supportive relationship with an adult (especially a non-abusive parent) can help protect children from the adverse effects of exposure to domestic abuse.

Very rarely will a mother tell you that the child witnessed or heard the abuse; usually she will say that the child was fast asleep in bed, or watching television and she had turned the sound up because she knew what was likely to happen. In reality, according to research, the child was either in the same or the next-door room when the abuse occurred.[9] Children are social beings, and just as when good things are happening in the home they want to be there, even when it's way past their bedtime, when bad things are happening, they want to be there too. Psychologists say that children as young as two start to feel responsible for their parents and want to protect them. We know that children will physically come between the perpetrator and the victim to protect their mummy. Children from a very young age will also try to protect their siblings.

Case example: Daniel Pelka's sibling

In the trial of Daniel Pelka's mother and stepfather for Daniel's murder, his sibling, whose age and gender have not been disclosed, told the court the following, according to reports in a local paper:[10]

> Talking about one incident – when Daniel was attacked while he was upstairs in a cold bath – the witness said Krezolek, the stepfather had had too much to drink. The child said: 'When [Krezolek] was too much drinking, my brother had a cold bath

---

9   Hughes, H. (1992) 'Impact of spouse abuse on children of battered women.' *Violence Update*, August, 1, 9–11.

10   Dimmer, S. (2013) 'Schoolboy murder trial: How I fought to save my brother Daniel.' *Coventry Telegraph*, 4 July. Available at www.coventrytelegraph.net/news/coventry-news/daniel-pelka-murder-trial-how-4866501

and I asked [Krezolek] to stop it. I got my brother from the bath and I pulled the plug out and I hugged him.'

Asked to give further details, the witness explained:

I was downstairs, I heard him screaming. I came upstairs and asked [Krezolek] to stop it, and he stopped it. I got my brother from the bath and put a towel on him and hugged him.

Asked what the witness thought about what had happened, the child said: 'I thought I needed to be brave to help my brother.' Describing another incident when Daniel was hurt by Krezolek, the witness said:

I was again brave and I pushed [Krezolek] to stop it and he stopped it. Then I checked my brother and I checked if he had got any marks and I saw loads [of] marks on him and I keep him safe. [Krezolek] didn't bother to look after him properly; he didn't even give him food or clean him.

On another occasion the witness recalled: 'I came back home, my brother was screaming. [Krezolek] was hitting him on his arms lots of times. I stopped him by kicking his legs. He said he hates me.'

Whatever the child's age, for a child to challenge, push and kick an adult male, who is brutal and at times drunk, or on drugs, is remarkable. There is a natural instinct to protect.

Case example: Natural instinct of a child to protect a younger sibling

In 2009, a mother was found guilty of neglect when she left her four children under the age of four for 24 hours while she went out partying. The trial received substantial media coverage at the time, and what was so stark and so poignant for many was that the police found toddler footprints in the powdered baby milk, where the four-year-old had tried to make a bottle for their three-month-old sibling.

In many cases, if professionals are gravely concerned about a child, they will try to encourage and support the mother to leave the partner, but it is worth remembering that the most dangerous time in the relationship is when a partner is planning to leave, or has just left.[11] The planning must be done jointly with those with expertise in domestic abuse, to ensure the safety of the woman and the child.

The way we tend to work in child protection when we are working with domestic abuse is that we focus on the mother, because she is seen as the protective parent, but what this does is reinforce to the mother that this is her problem, her fault. As described in Chapter 1, we know that perpetrators often tell victims that social care is only involved because they are so useless, and every meeting the mother has with social care and other agencies confirms that. No matter how sensitively we deal with a situation, what we are saying to that mother is that we are involved because we are so concerned about her children, and because she is the primary carer, and is not doing her job properly.

We need to find a way to work more effectively with the perpetrator of the violence. The first place to start is to seek advice from your local domestic abuse service about how to do that, on a case-by-case basis. Those working in child protection would greatly benefit from more advice and guidance generally from specialist domestic abuse organisations, because in my experience, we focus on the mother as we do not really know what to do about the man, and that is wrong.

Case example: Too great a focus on the mother

When I was a frontline social worker we had a case that came in from a domestic abuse charity. It was a horrific domestic abuse case, but the mother kept reassuring everyone that her three-year-old son did not see anything, that she could definitely keep him safe, and that there was nothing to worry about.

The charity had to meet with the mother while her partner was at work, as he had no idea she was receiving support, and she knew

11 Saunders, H. (2004) *Twenty-Nine Child Homicides: Lessons Still To Be Learnt on Domestic Violence and Child Protection.* Bristol: Women's Aid Federation of England (WAFE).

he would react adversely if he found out. The charity and the mother had a very complex way of communicating, so he never found out.

The charity said that the mother was a professional woman, who worked from home. She was the main breadwinner and was very intelligent and articulate.

It was agreed that I would go and meet the mother, in a shopping centre, so her partner's suspicions would not be raised.

I went to meet her, and sure enough, she was clearly intelligent and articulate, and told me all about her safety plans if anything were to happen with her child – she had it all planned. She said that if her partner knew that social care was involved, and if we were to even think about a child protection conference, that would put her and her child at great risk. She was not in a place where she would consider leaving her partner, and she said she could manage the situation.

I went back to the office and discussed it with my manager. We both agreed that we would put the child at greater risk if we got involved, and because this mother was so convincing about her ability to protect her child, we closed the case.

This case has always haunted me. How much were we persuaded by the fact that she was clearly an intelligent woman, who presented a very good argument as to why she could manage the situation, when the reality was, that her partner was 6ft 2" and a very violent man, and she was only 5ft 4" and there was a three-year-old child? And that only takes into consideration the physical risk to the child; it overlooks the emotional impact on the child of witnessing and hearing domestic abuse.

There are now some community perpetrator programmes, but they are not available in every area, and there are always issues around funding because these are delivered by the voluntary sector. But at least it is a step in the right direction.

Professionals deal with conundrums like the one set out above every single day. The starting point for whether social care should become involved should be the question, 'Is the child suffering, or likely to suffer, significant harm as a result of maltreatment?' If the answer to that is 'yes', social care has a duty to respond. The question, 'Do we have the right processes and services in place to improve children's lives?' is a different question, but it should not be one that that stops social care becoming involved.

Substance misuse

Language

We hear the terms 'using substances', 'misusing substances' and 'substance abuse', but what is the difference?

Some people are able to use recreational or prescription drugs without ever experiencing negative consequences, for themselves or their children, or addiction. They are users of substances, in whatever form. This may not impact negatively on children in the home.

For many others, substance use can cause problems, although use does not automatically lead to abuse, and there is no specific level at which drug use moves from casual to problematic. It varies for each individual. The terms 'drug abuse' and 'drug misuse' are more to do with the consequences of drug use. No matter how often or how little someone is consuming, if their drug use is causing problems in their life – at work, school, home or in their relationships – they are likely to have a drug abuse or addiction problem. This will always impact negatively on children in the home.

Do 'substances' include alcohol? 'Yes' is the answer, and although alcohol is a drug, many people also refer to 'drugs and alcohol', to separate out the two.

Some facts and figures

> Forty-seven per cent of violent crime is linked to alcohol.[12]

> Forty-two per cent of serious case reviews between 2009–11 featured substance misuse.[13]

---

12 Office for National Statistics (2013) 'Crime Statistics, Nature of Crime Tables, 2011/12.' Available at www.ons.gov.uk/ons/publications/re-reference-tables.html?edition=tcm%3A77-296029

13 Brandon, M., Sidebotham, P., Bailey, S., Belderson, P., Hawley, C., Ellis, C. and Megson, M. (2012) *New Learning from Serious Case Reviews: A Two Year Report for 2009–11*. London: Department for Education. Available at www.gov.uk/government/uploads/system/uploads/attachment_data/file/184053/DFE-RR226_Report.pdf

> › Nearly one in three children (30 per cent) live with at least one parent who is a binge drinker (between 3.3–3.5 million children).

> › A fifth (22 per cent) live with a hazardous drinker (over 2.5 million children).

> › Around 79,000 babies under the age of one in England are living with a parent who is classified as a 'problematic' drinker ('hazardous' or 'harmful'). This is equivalent to 93,500 babies in the UK.

> › Around 26,000 babies under the age of one in England are living with a parent who would be classified as a 'dependent' drinker. This is equivalent to 31,000 across the UK.[14]

> › Parental substance misuse is a significant factor in up to two-thirds of all care proceedings and, according to a London survey, was the most frequent parental factor in long-term children and family social work, affecting 34 per cent of all cases.[15]

In 2003 the Advisory Council for the Misuse of Drugs produced a report on children of parents misusing substances. The report was called *Hidden Harm*.[16] It estimated that at that time there were between 250,000 and 350,000 children of problem drug users in the UK.

---

14 Children's Commissioner (2012) Silent Voices: Supporting children and young people affected by parental misuse. Available at www.childrenscommissioner. gov.uk/sites/default/files/publications/Silent%20Voices%20key%20briefing. pdf

15 Munro, E. (2011) *The Munro Review of Child Protection: Final Report. A Child-Centred System.* London: Department for Education. Available at www. gov.uk/government/uploads/system/uploads/attachment_data/file/175391/ Munro-Review.pdf

16 Advisory Council for the Misuse of Drugs (2003) Hidden Harm. Available at www.gov.uk/government/uploads/system/uploads/attachment_ data/file/120620/hidden-harm-full.pdf

In 2012 the Office of the Children's Commissioner produced a report called *Silent Voices. Supporting Children and Young People Affected by Parental Alcohol Misuse*. Their view was: 'The current family-focused agenda does not address parental alcohol misuse at a strategic level. There is a lack of alcohol specific focus. Similarly, there is less recognition, and response, to alcohol misuse, compared to drugs misuse.'

Parents who are using street drugs or misusing alcohol are unlikely to be honest with professionals about the extent of their alcohol or drug dependency because of the illegality and social stigma around drugs, and a fear of having their children removed, and too often professionals take what the parent says at face value. This can result in professionals underestimating the impact on the child of the substance misuse. We also see from some serious case reviews that if a mother is misusing heroin, the focus of child protection professionals is on that, rather than considering the wider impact of the mother mixing heroin with other drugs, and what that might mean in terms of how it might impair her parenting capacity.

Just as with domestic abuse, child protection workers cannot expect to be experts in this area and know all the details of all the drugs and the common effects of each of them, and that is why it is so important to make sure they work closely with the substance misuse service – and get advice from the experts.

Foetal alcohol spectrum disorder[17]

Foetal alcohol spectrum disorder is the umbrella term for a range of alcohol-related birth defects.

We do not know how alcohol might affect an unborn baby. It could have different effects at different times during pregnancy, and it might affect one baby but not another, but what we do know is that we are seeing an increasing number of babies born with a foetal alcohol disorder.

---

17 www.nofas-uk.org/documents/2011.331%20NOFAS%20Factsheets%20 Generic%20Final.pdf

We know that alcohol is a teratogen – a substance that interferes with the development of the embryo or foetus. Whereas an adult liver can filter out the toxins, the foetus's liver is not able to do so. Instead, the alcohol circulates in the foetus's blood system. It can kill brain cells and damage the nervous system of the foetus throughout the entire nine months of pregnancy.

Foetal alcohol syndrome is the most clinically recognisable form of foetal alcohol spectrum disorder, seen in approximately 20 per cent of cases. It is diagnosed based on the presence of a characteristic set of facial features, combined with growth and neurocognitive defects. These may include small, wide-set eye openings, a flattened philtrum (the area between the nose and the upper lip), thin upper lip, lower ears, different creases in the hands, and there can be skeletal damage.

There are other forms of foetal alcohol spectrum disorder: alcohol-related neurodevelopmental disorder, alcohol-related birth defects, foetal alcohol effects and partial foetal alcohol syndrome. (Just to confuse things, in the US, foetal alcohol spectrum disorder is known as foetal alcohol syndrome, and only one other form of the disorder is labelled, and that is foetal alcohol effects, which is not as severe as foetal alcohol syndrome.)

There are also a number of invisible foetal alcohol spectrum disorder characteristics, which may include:

› attention deficits

› memory deficits

› hyperactivity

› difficulty with abstract concepts (e.g. maths, time and money)

› poor problem-solving skills

› difficulty learning from consequences

› poor judgement

› immature behaviour

› poor impulse control

› confused social skills.

The number of diagnosed cases in England of foetal alcohol syndrome in babies born to women who drink during pregnancy has tripled since records of the debilitating condition were first kept, 16 years ago.

In 2012–13 there were 252 diagnoses of the syndrome, compared with 89 in 1997–98. Cases are up 37 per cent since 2009–10.[18]

One of the challenges with foetal alcohol spectrum disorder is that if a baby is removed from its mother because of her alcohol addiction, we cannot tell the possible future long-term carers of the child, whether that be extended family or adopters, what the likely impact will be on the child. Unless it is clearly a case of foetal alcohol syndrome and the physical signs can be seen, we will not know the effect on the child until the child develops, and even if we can say definitively at a young age that the baby has foetal alcohol syndrome, we cannot say what the neurological impact will be. This can make these babies hard to place in long-term care.

When mothers are using other drugs during pregnancy it is not so clear-cut. There are many different types of drugs, stimulants, hallucinogens and opiates, and many women will use a variety of drugs, known as polydrug use. This makes it difficult for researchers to separate out the effects of each on the unborn baby.

The other factor is environmental, which goes back to the nature/nurture debate. It is very difficult to be clear if children are the way they are because of their environment.

Newborn babies of opiate-using mothers may go through withdrawal, which consists of central nervous system and digestive system symptoms that may include irritability, poor feeding, poor weight gain, ineffective sucking, yawning, sneezing and

---

18 Boffey, D. (2014) 'Sharp rise in babies born with foetal alcohol syndrome.' *The Guardian*, 21 June. Available at www.theguardian.com/society/2014/jun/21/pregnant-women-alcohol-abuse

tremulousness, and sometimes seizures. They are often of low birth weight and have a small head circumference, which can be associated with increased risk for later developmental problems. Most withdrawal symptoms disappear by two months, but the irritability may persist during the first year or longer, contributing to caretaking difficulties similar to those encountered by parents of cocaine-affected infants.

Low birth weight, growth delay in utero and small-sized heads at birth are all potential consequences of cocaine use during pregnancy. With respect to behaviour, cocaine-exposed newborn babies do not all react in the same way. It is not known why that is, or why some babies show the symptoms with greater intensity and persistence than others.

Immediately after birth, some cocaine-exposed babies are often in great distress. Jittery and suffering tremors, the babies are irritable and sensitive to the mildest environmental stimulation. Their muscles are unusually stiff, and they may show a prolonged persistence of early reflexes. Often, they cry a great deal. They do not fall asleep readily, but once asleep are easily awakened. The distress of these newborns is clear, but they are unable to calm themselves. However, sometimes cocaine-exposed babies display the opposite characteristics – they sleep much of the time, and appear to shut down as if to avoid environmental stimulation.

Although the problems associated with motor development, such as increased muscle tone and persistence of reflexes, usually diminish during the first year, irritability, sleep and feeding problems, and difficulty with calming, may continue into the second year for some infants.[19]

---

19 Kronstadt, D. (1991) 'Complex developmental issues of prenatal drug exposure.' *Drug-Exposed Infants* 1(1). Available at www.princeton.edu/futureofchildren/publications/journals/article/index.xml?journalid=69&articleid=499&sectionid=3394

Mental ill health

Mental illness is on a spectrum – it may be very mild, such as someone who is feeling low, through to someone whose illness is so severe they are unable to care for themselves and may pose a danger to themselves or others.

Language

Why do some people talk about 'mental health problems' and others talk of 'mental illness'? What is the difference?

'Mental health problems' is more of a generic term that covers the whole spectrum, from mildly depressed or anxious, to severe mental illnesses.

Some facts and figures

> It is thought that approximately 68 per cent of mothers and 57 per cent of fathers have a mental illness;[20] however, there are no national requirements to gather information and report on the number of parents who have serious mental health difficulties, and therefore only estimates can be made. In the words of Ofsted's report, *What About the Children?*[21], 'In the absence of any national drivers there is limited scrutiny of this issue within mental health services generally.'

REMEMBER...

As we said in Chapter 1, mental illness in a parent does not equal maltreatment of a child.

---

20 Royal College of Psychiatrists (no date) Mental Health and Growing Up Factsheet. 'Parental mental illness: the impact on children and adolescents: information for parents, carers and anyone who works with young people.' Available at www.rcpsych.ac.uk/healthadvice/parentsandyouthinfo/parentscarers/parentalmentalillness.aspx

21 Ofsted (2013) What About the Children? Available at http://dera.ioe.ac.uk/17492/1/What%20about%20the%20children.pdf

›   Information about the number of parents with mental ill health is often not collected at a local level either, and so most of the evidence of the links between mental ill health and child deaths or significant injuries comes from serious case reviews, bearing in mind how commonly it is linked to substance misuse and domestic abuse.

›   In the serious case review data from 2009–11 there was a 10 per cent rise in deliberate homicides. A number of these were women suffering from postpartum depression killing their babies.

›   In nearly 60 per cent of serious case reviews between 2009–11 mental illness was a factor.[22]

›   According to the report there is some evidence that adult mental health workers do not recognise and analyse the impact of the adult's mental ill health on the children. It was found that 'the majority of assessments of children where parents or carers had mental health difficulties did not provide a comprehensive and reflective analysis of the impact of their mental ill health on the child.'

›   Although there is a clear requirement of any professional, including mental health workers, that if they have concerns about a child they must respond, if child protection is not high up on the national agenda, in terms of adult mental health, it is understandable that workers on the front line are not as attuned to it as drug and alcohol workers.

22 Brandon, M., Sidebotham, P., Bailey, S., Belderson, P., Hawley, C., Ellis, C. and Megson, M. (2012) *New Learning from Serious Case Reviews: A Two Year Report for 2009–11*. London: Department for Education. Available at www.gov.uk/government/uploads/system/uploads/attachment_data/file/184053/DFE-RR226_Report.pdf

› This can also work the other way round – child protection workers can underestimate the impact of the illness, adversely affecting the parenting capacity of the parent. This is why, as with all other professionals, it is essential that mental health workers and child protection workers work closely together, for each to gain a greater understanding, which will ultimately result in greater protection for children.

› There may be many reasons why a parent does not seek help with a mental health problem. We have looked at this in some depth in Chapter 1, but it is important that when you are working with a family where there is mental ill health, that you understand what is happening, and why it is happening. For example, over the years I have worked with several men who have been diagnosed with schizophrenia but who refused to take their medication because the drug they were prescribed made them impotent.

Case example: Refusing medication

Tom came from a loving family with no history of mental illness. When he was 23 he was diagnosed with schizophrenia. He had been hearing voices, and to combat this he had been smoking cannabis and misusing alcohol – he said that this was the only thing that quietened the voices that were telling him what to do all the time. Tom was very ill and unable to work.

After Tom was diagnosed he was prescribed medication, which he took for a while, but then he got together with a girlfriend. One of the side effects of the medication was that it meant Tom had problems with impotence, and as a 23-year-old man he did not want that, so he stopped taking his medication.

Tom went on to have two children with his partner. He was always strongly encouraged to take his medication and he would usually say he had, but in truth, we never knew. Because of Tom's illness and his self-medicating with cannabis and alcohol, it was not safe to have him around the children unsupervised. The strain became too much for his partner, and she left him.

From that time onwards Tom had intermittent contact with his children, whom he clearly loved very much. Tragically, his drug and alcohol addiction took over his life and he died at a young age.

As with almost all of the parents we work with in child protection, Tom was not a 'bad' man. In this case he was an extremely vulnerable adult who was very unwell.

Why the link between the three?

There is a very strong link between all three factors because a woman who is a victim of domestic abuse may very well develop mental health problems as a result of the fear she lives with every day of her life, as well as the strain of having to pretend to other people that nothing is happening – the secrecy, the shame that victims are made to feel because the perpetrator will always tell the victim it is their fault (and if you are told something enough you believe it), as well as trying to keep children safe.

A woman is more likely to turn to substances, usually alcohol, as a coping mechanism when she is a victim of domestic abuse. In addition to this is the behaviour of the perpetrator. Although, as stated in Chapter 1, alcohol is not a trigger for violence, it is a disinhibitor. We know that 47 per cent of violent crime is linked to alcohol, and between 16 and 25 per cent of all violent crime is domestic abuse. We also know that some people who have mental health problems self-medicate, as with the case example above – you then have an undiagnosed or untreated mental health problem combined with substance abuse, and that is a potent mix.

The purpose of Ofsted's 2013 report *What About the Children?*[23] was to explore how well adult mental health services and drug and alcohol services considered the impact on children when their parents had mental ill health and/or drug and alcohol problems, and how effectively adult and children's services worked together

23 Ofsted (2013) What About the Children? Available at http://dera.ioe. ac.uk/17492/1/What%20about%20the%20children.pdf

to ensure that children affected by their parents' difficulties were supported and safe. It found that drug and alcohol workers had a better understanding of the needs of the children than the adult mental health workers. If we refer back to the facts and figures of this section above, this is understandable. There is more in the public and professional arena about the links between substance misuse and child maltreatment than there is about the links between mental ill health and child maltreatment.

There is often a great deal of shame and secrecy around domestic abuse, mental ill health and substance misuse, and children may be told from an early age that they must not talk about it – if they tell anyone, they will be taken away, daddy will go to prison etc., and so children do not speak of what is happening at home.

Case example: Living with a secret

Sam was living with his mother, father and siblings. There was domestic abuse, and both parents were using street drugs. Life was very chaotic for the children, even though the parents did a very good job of presenting as a 'normal' family. For years no one picked up on what was happening in the home.

Sam's mother told the children that there was only one thing worse than a pit bull terrier, and that was a social worker. She also told them that if they breathed a word of what was going on at home, they would be taken away from her and would never see her again.

In this chapter we have looked at each of these factors in their own right, in the context of child protection. We have talked of the 'toxic trio' when you see all three together, but it does not necessarily go from one to all three. In some families there will be domestic abuse and mental ill health, but not substance misuse; in other words, there can be any variant of these factors. What we know is that risks increase exponentially when there is one or more of these factors in a child's life.

We have also talked about the secrecy element of each of these factors, so how can we, as workers seeing a family for an hour or so in their home or our offices, maybe once a week, or once every two weeks, ever really know what is going on? The answer is, realistically, in some cases we will never know, but there is certainly much we can do to try to ascertain what is going on:

> › If you think there are things going on that are being hidden from you, visit the home when the family are not expecting you. In Chapter 5 we look at home visiting in greater depth, but for now, take in everything in your environment. If there are concerns of violence, check out the state of the home.

Case example: Building evidence

One of my most satisfying moments in court was when I, a social worker, disagreed with an eminent 'expert witness' to almost audible gasps in the court.

One of the aspects of the court case was whether the father could have unsupervised contact with his baby son, which is what he wanted. It was my view, supported by my manager, that he should not be allowed unsupervised contact because he was misusing cannabis and alcohol, and he could be extremely violent.

As part of the care proceedings the expert witness had interviewed the father twice, and he had told him that he was no longer using cannabis and he only had the odd drink. He also said the same thing to the 'voluntary' substance misuse service he was told to engage with as part of the court proceedings. On the basis of this, the expert witness had recommended that he be allowed unsupervised contact.

The difference between the expert witness's evidence and mine was that he had never been to the home and seen the punch marks in the door and the walls, and the cuts and bruises on the father's knuckles. He had not smelt the strong smell of cannabis every time you entered the home, and had not spoken to the paternal grandmother who was so frightened of her son she stayed in her bedroom all day until he went out.

I am happy to say that the judge went with our recommendation. It was the right thing for the child, which is all that matters at the end of the day.

> › Speak to the child. It is shocking how often children are overlooked. They will usually know much more about what is going on than anyone gives them credit for. Make sure

you allay their fears. Children are often frightened they can 'catch' the mental illness their parent suffers from – they may be frightened they are going to be a drug addict too, they may be frightened you are only asking them because you are going to take them away. We have looked in greater depth at communicating with children in Chapter 2, but remember never to be critical of the child's parent. This will never help a child and will put barriers up, not break them down.

> Be very clear with the family that you are there to help and support families, and only a tiny percentage of children are ever taken into care, which will be their greatest fear.

> Work very closely with the other professionals. It is surprising how parents often give one person one bit of information and another something else. Put all the pieces of the puzzle together to try to build up the best picture you can.

> Work with the extended family, where relevant and where possible.

Case example: Ask the family

A maternal grandfather said to me once, 'No one ever asked us.' This was a case where both of the parents had used and misused drugs for years. Their children were on and off child protection plans and were eventually taken into care, to be placed with another family member. During the time they were living with the parents, the family often stayed with the maternal grandparents, who took on a lot of the caring role, but their view was that they were invisible to the professionals, except in terms of caring for the children, taking them to appointments, and later supervising contact.

The slogan goes, 'Think child. Think adult. Think family', and that is exactly what we should all be doing, wherever we work. Always ask yourself, 'What is the impact on the child of the adult's life?', and if you do not know the answer, ask someone who does.

5 Home Visiting

Carrying out home visits is one of the most important areas of our work, which is why I have written a whole book on the subject.[1] This chapter looks at why it matters so much.

The reason why it is so important is because the home is where we will get the greatest sense of what life is like for the child, and how safe the child may be. A key aspect of any child protection investigation should be your visits to the family home, but it can be the hardest environment to work in – there can be all sorts of distractions, and sometimes threats, and any professional will feel more vulnerable in the family home than they would meeting the family in their office, but none of that should ever stop you spending time in the family home. It is unsurprising that what we see from serious case reviews and public inquiries is that the evidence is often before our eyes, when we are in a family home. We just have to know where to look, and what to do.

Every family we visit will be different. Of course not every family we visit will be hostile, not every home will have an aggressive dog, or 15 people sitting in the kitchen, but a significant number of families we visit will not want us there, and that is completely understandable. How many of you would want a stranger inviting themselves into your home, particularly if you thought they had the power to remove your children?

As with all of our work, we must never make assumptions. Do not assume that the angry father, whose house is very untidy, is abusing his child, but the warm and friendly mother, with the spotless home who ushers you in and makes you tea, is not. Look beneath the surface. Often people are angry because they are afraid.

---

1   Nicolas, J. (2012) *Conducting the Home Visit in Child Protection*. Maidenhead: Open University Press.

Maybe they are afraid because we are going to find out what they have been doing, but maybe they are just afraid because they love their child so much and they are terrified of our power, and the only way they know to show that fear is by shouting.

This brings me on to my final point before we consider the specifics of home visits – power. Never forget the imbalance of power and that, however reluctantly, that family has let you into their home, and we must never abuse that position.

Preparing for the visit

It is really important that you are well prepared. Ask yourself the following questions:

> What is the reason for this visit?

> What do I need to get from the visit?

> Have I got all the information I need before I do the visit?

The better prepared you are, the more you will achieve. When I reflect on my practice I can recall visits where I realise that beyond ticking the box saying 'Family seen', I did not actually achieve anything at all. Make sure you read the file and speak to other professionals before you visit. We all rush around saying we are far too busy, but if we spent more time preparing, it would save us time in the long run.

If it is your first visit to the family, think about the practicalities – will you be able to find the flat or house? Satellite navigation is great, but will it take you to a huge estate, or a dead-end lane in the middle of nowhere and tell you that you have reached your destination?

Think about language – does the family speak English? If not, do you need to take an interpreter? Find out from professionals already working with the family, and be prepared. It is a waste of time to arrive at someone's home and then find out that they do not speak English.

Think about safety – are there any concerns? Should you go with someone else? We do joint visits for all sorts of reasons – sometimes because it feels safer, but sometimes it is because we want a fresh pair of eyes. Sometimes we may do joint visits to show the family that we are working together and they cannot play one professional off against another. If you are doing a joint visit, plan with your colleague beforehand how the visit will run and what you need to cover, and have a plan for what to do if you feel threatened. (If your reason for doing a joint visit is safety, ask yourself, 'If I don't feel safe visiting this home alone, why is okay for the child to live there?')

Think about what you wear to work, in the context of when you are visiting people's homes. Do not wear a short skirt if there is a toddler and you will be sitting on the floor playing. Do not wear your daughter's Disney socks and then realise that you are going to be asked to take your boots off. Wear clothes that will wash easily, as we cannot get away from the fact that some of the homes we go into are in a poor state. So wear things you can throw in the wash when you get home, and then you can concentrate on what really matters – the child.

Getting in the door

If you think the family is likely to try to evade you, park your car around the corner. In some of the areas we visit, professionals are very conspicuous. Be sensitive to the family – they may not want their neighbours' attention drawn to the fact that they have a professional visiting.

When you knock on the door, if the person who answers is not the person you are there to see, if they ask, just tell them your first name and that you are from the council, nothing more. If the person you have come to see is called and comes to the door, but the other person is still there, tell them who you are and that you are from the council, but do not say any more without checking that the service user is happy to have the discussion in front of someone else. When you know you are speaking to the right person, always show them your identification.

If you are visiting someone who you think will try and evade you, and they live in a block of flats, walk around the side of the building. Ring someone else's bell and ask if they could let you in because you have a letter for Number X. People usually let you in, or if there is one, ring the trades bell. Before you knock on the door of the flat you are visiting, again, listen at the door to see if you hear voices or activity. Sometimes you can hear voices from within but it all goes quiet when you knock on the door, and no one will open it.

It's at that point that I start talking through the letter box (beware of dogs!) – my usual starting point will be, 'It's Joanna here, from the council. I need to talk to you and I would rather not say what I have to say from out here because this is your private business. Please would you let me in?' Many people realise at this point that it will be less awful to let me in than to have me shouting out their business from the landing.

You always have to make a judgement as to whether you feel it is safe to go into the home. Never go in if you feel unsafe.

If you have had no response to your calling through the letterbox, you will have to leave, but it is important to put in your recording that you heard noises in the flat before you knocked, and that it then went quiet. It all helps to build a picture.

If you are unable to gain entry to a home for any reason, your first thought must be about the child you went to see. What is the level of risk to that child? Do you need to report straight back to your manager that you were unable to see the child? (This will depend on the level of risk.) For example, if you are doing the first home visit to a four-day-old baby who is the subject of a child protection plan following a pre-birth child protection conference, and you are unable to see the baby, this must be taken very seriously. Always weigh up the risk to the child when considering your next course of action, and always record when you have been unable to see the child.

When I was at university no one told us what to do if, when the door is opened and you have introduced yourself with a friendly smile, the person tells you to 'F*** off' and slams the door. So what do you do? The bottom line is that you have to 'F*** off' because there is not much else you can do, but everything that happens when you are working with a family should inform your assessment, for better or for worse. In that situation you have to weigh up what you think the level of risk is to the child. I would suggest you tell your manager and discuss the situation with them.

Other situations you may be faced with

Certain pets can be threatening, and it is completely reasonable to ask the family to put the pet away, as long as you bear in mind it is their home. If they are not intentionally using the pet to make you feel threatened, they should not mind.

Case example: Difficult conversation

I was involved in a case where the family had a number of snakes. They were kept in tanks in the front room, but were often let out, and that was always the room they took me into. Someone often answered the door with a snake wrapped round them.

There was no way I could concentrate with snakes writhing around, so on my first visit I asked if we could talk in the kitchen instead, with no snakes on anyone. The family resisted, and I definitely got the feeling that they had the snakes out for my benefit.

I explained to them that I would not be able to concentrate, and what I was there about was really important, and I hoped they thought it was really important too, because I was there about X, their child, and it would be really helpful if we went into the kitchen. I did say that it did not matter what state the kitchen was in.

After my first visit I made it very clear that it would be very helpful if future meetings could be in the kitchen.

In an extreme case the family might say that it is their house and that it is up to them where their pet is. In that case you need to be more assertive, and I would suggest this as a response, 'I am sorry, but I do need to speak to you today, but I am very wary of snakes and I won't be able to come in if you will not put the snakes in another room just while I am here. Can I just be clear? Are you saying you are not prepared to do that?'

If the family still refuses, I would say, 'I am sorry but I am not going to come in if you are not willing to put your pet away. I am going to go now, and my office will be in touch.'

A child answers the door

When the door is answered by a child, the first thing to do is to ask if their mummy/daddy is there. What happens next will depend on the child's response and age. If the child says, 'Daddy's asleep and mummy's gone' and it is a young child, I would ask if they could be very clever and go and wake daddy up, while I wait on the doorstep. If they come back and say they cannot wake him, you need to ensure that both father and child are alright. If you feel it may be unsafe to enter the home, ring the police and stay there with the child until the police arrive. If you have no concerns for your personal safety, go into the home with the child, calling the father's name loudly. If he is in a bedroom, knock on the door loudly and call his name until he wakes up.

Case example: Difficulty getting in

I was visiting the home of two children who were the subject of child protection plans – Dani, aged three-and-a-half, and Maya, aged nine months. The concern was neglect. The home was in a poor state, and the children often did not make it to the children's centre or to medical appointments. They lived with their mother, and there was a concern that she was leaving them alone to go and meet strange men in bars. There was also a concern that she was bringing these strangers home. She had not been clinically diagnosed as being an alcoholic, but we knew she was a binge drinker.

Part of the child protection plan was that we would do unannounced home visits, which is what I was doing on this occasion. It was 4 o'clock in the afternoon. When I got to the flat I could hear loud music. I knocked on the door and as I knocked, it swung open a little. I held it closed and knocked again. Dani then opened the door, looking very wary. I knelt down and asked her if her mummy was at home. She just nodded. I asked her if she could be very clever and go and get mummy for me. She shook her head. I said I really needed to talk to mummy, so it would be really kind if she went to get her. For the first time Dani spoke, and said, 'I can't. Mummy in her room with her friend. Mummy says not allowed go in. Naughty. Mummy smack me.' I could hear Maya, the baby, crying. I asked where Maya was. Dani said, 'Maya on floor. Maya crying.'

So then I had a dilemma. My instinct was to go in, shouting to alert the mother and her companion to my entrance, but I had no idea if the 'friend' was male or female, and I was also aware they might be very angry if I just went in and I was potentially putting myself at great risk.

So what I did was ring 999. I told the police the situation, and they said they would be there in five minutes. Maya seemed to be getting more distressed, so I told the police I was going to go in and to please get there as soon as possible.

I went into the flat, calling all the time. The music in the bedroom was pounding and the door was shut. Maya was lying on the floor in the front room. There was a baby's bottle lying next to her and next to that an empty bottle of vodka. I picked Maya up and said to Dani, 'Look! I want to show you something!' I took her hand and took them both to the entrance to the flat, desperately thinking what I could show them. (My thinking was I did not want to bang on the bedroom door and shout to get the mother's attention because I thought that would frighten Maya and possibly Dani, and I knew the police were on their way.)

I knelt in the door of the flat, holding Maya, with Dani on my knee, and opened my bag. I was hoping Dani would like the games on my phone. I made a big show of getting it out, and Dani helped choose which app to open – this was all just stalling tactics until the police got there.

The police arrived very quickly and they went into the flat. There was no answer to their knocking on the bedroom door, so they opened it. The mother and a man were lying on the bed naked. The mother had passed out and the man was very drunk.

The children were taken into police protection and I had to take them to an emergency foster placement. Those children never went home again.

As always, you have to make a judgement. If there is no adult there, is the child old enough to be left alone? (There is no legal age that a child can be left alone – it depends entirely on the child and the circumstances.) Is it safe for you to enter the home? Should you call the police? Should you ring your manager for advice? These are your options, and you will have to make the decision based on the evidence you have.

The person answering the door does not speak English

Once you know the person doesn't speak English, repeat the name of the person you are there to see. You could also write the name down. If you get nowhere with this, you will have to leave. In the office, find out more about the family; if you are not sure you have the right address, talk to your local housing department. They are a wealth of knowledge.

If the person you are there to see comes to the door but they do not speak English, you could either try saying 'English?' and gesticulating into the home. In other words, is there anyone there who speaks English? If no one is forthcoming, you will have to return with an interpreter. If someone else comes forward who does speak English, first of all, establish who they are and whether they are either any relation to the children or the primary carer. If they are not, I would give away very little information. Ask to see the children and then, depending on the circumstances, explain that you will return with an interpreter. Try to agree a time with the primary carer then, as it will be difficult to communicate by telephone later.

As in all cases, your decision will depend on the urgency and purpose of your visit.

Once in the home

The first thing is to establish who is in the room, and who will remain for the interview. You are there to do a job. If the room is full of people, you must say to the person you are there to see that you need to talk to them, but would not want to do so with so many others in the room. Ask if you can you talk to them somewhere private. If the person says it is fine in front of everyone, insist, and say something like, 'I'm sorry, but I am not happy to talk about your business in front of so many people. I need to talk to you privately.' In my experience the parent will generally accede, even if it is with some huffing and puffing. If not, make a judgement call, depending on the urgency and purpose of your visit. It may be best to make an appointment for the parent to come into the office, and during that visit explain that when you go to their home, you will need to see them alone.

You will now be beginning to get an impression of what it might be like for the child living in this home, which will become a vital part of your assessment.

Gaining access to the rest of the house

Just as social workers do not have right of entry to a property, neither do they have the right to look around the home without the parents' consent, but we cannot do a thorough assessment of the child's situation if we have not seen where they sleep, eat and bathe. It is essential, when we are visiting a home as part of a child protection investigation, that we see the child's environment. Do not automatically be suspicious if a family is reluctant to let you go upstairs, or in the bedrooms and the bathroom, however. Put yourself in their shoes – how would you feel if the health visitor asked to see your bedrooms, for example? But you do, nonetheless, need to see the child's living conditions.

Case example: Daniel Pelka's living conditions

What came to light during the criminal trial was that Daniel was allegedly kept locked in a boxroom over a period of several months. The door handle had been removed. The police described there being a very thin mattress on the floor, but no furniture and no toys – just some very thin threadbare carpet, which was heavily urine-stained. There was no heating and no pictures on the walls, and it was a bitterly cold winter the winter before Daniel died. It is believed that when Daniel was not at school, he was kept locked in this room.

If any professional had done an unannounced visit and seen the whole house, they would have seen this, and there may have been a different outcome. There are many ifs and buts, in these horrific cases of children being killed. Do not underestimate the power of the unannounced visit, when you can see the whole house.

I am not suggesting that as soon as you enter the home you tell the parent or carer that you need to see the entire house – that would be insensitive and poor practice – but if you are doing a child protection visit, or you are doing a parenting assessment, or you are a family worker and you have not yet seen the bedrooms, kitchen, front room and bathroom, you need to do so, or record clearly why the parent is not willing to let you see the rest of the home.

Only ask to see the rest of the home once you have had a conversation with the family and hopefully built up some kind of rapport with them. I am not suggesting that any of this work is easy, and it can be very difficult to ask someone if you can see their bedrooms, kitchen and bathroom, and then whether you can look in their fridge and their cupboards, but it needs to be done.

What to look out for
Case example: Putting on a front

Several years ago I worked with a family, and there were huge concerns about the children being malnourished – at school they were always taking food from other children's lunch boxes and from the kitchen.

Every time the social worker or family support worker visited the home, the parents would show them cupboards full of food. No one could understand what was going on.

Then one day the family support worker went to pick up a tin, to see what was behind it. The tin was empty and so were all the rest, as were the packets of food. The parents had also stacked the empty cans and packets up at the front of the cupboard, but there was nothing behind them.

It taught us all a lesson. You have to check absolutely everything.

REMEMBER...

Do not overlook the bathroom. Victoria Climbié was kept in the bath, and it is often the place where poor hygiene is evident.

Seeing a sleeping baby

When you visit a home, if you are told that you cannot see the baby because the baby is asleep, think of your role. If you are there in a child protection capacity, then you absolutely need to see the baby. Remember that it is the under-ones who are the most vulnerable and at greatest risk of death, and if you are there as part of a risk assessment, you must see the baby. I would just explain this to the primary carer, and it may be that you are satisfied by standing at the bedroom door, where you can see that the baby is asleep and breathing.

As always, it is how we deliver things that makes all the difference. If we are respectful and honest with families, we will work much more constructively than if we abuse our position and laud it over the families we work with.

Observing how the adults and children interact

There is a considerable amount of research that tells us of the importance of a child having a primary carer who is able to prioritise their child's needs above their own, and this now forms the basis of attachment theory, which was first defined by John Bowlby in the 1940s, and went on to be developed by Mary Ainsworth, in particular, as well as many others.[2,3,4] As part of our assessment it is essential we ascertain whether the child we are working with has this positive attachment, but I would add a note of caution here. Do not use the term 'attachment' unless you are an expert in attachment theory, which most of us, including me, are not. Describe exactly what it is you are seeing: 'I have never seen the mother respond when her baby stirs, or starts to make noises, whether they are gurgling, or

---

2   Bowlby, J. (1951) *Maternal Care and Mental Health.* Geneva: World Health Organization.

3   Ainsworth, M.D.S. (1968) 'Object relations, dependency, and attachment: A theoretical review of the infant mother relationship.' *Child Development* 40, 969–1025.

4   Ainsworth, M.D.S., Bell, S.M. and Stayton, D. (1974) 'Infant-Mother Attachment and Social Development.' In M.P. Richards (ed.) *The Introduction of the Child into a Social World* (pp.99–135). London: Cambridge University Press.

whimpering. I have never seen her make eye contact with her baby.' This will tell you an awful lot more than 'X has a poor attachment.'

Observe how the adults in the home respond to the child. Does the mother respond to the baby's cry? Does the primary carer just stick the dummy back in, without looking at the baby, and continue talking about her own problems? Does anyone pick the baby up and soothe them? Does the baby ever make a noise? (Babies learn very quickly that it is a waste of energy to cry if no one responds, but remember that there may be an organic reason for their silence. As always, consider the context.) Does the child look to the mother for reassurance, which is very natural in a young child, or does the child come straight to you and climb on your knee? Does the child seem frightened, or watchful? Is the primary carer controlling the interview? (What comes from many serious case reviews is that the parents have been calling the shots and have been controlling not just over their children but also, very subtly sometimes, over the professionals too.)

What is the atmosphere like? It may be understandably tense because you are there, but in addition to that, we can learn a lot from how a child responds to a parent, or the adults in the home, becoming upset or angry. Is the child emotionless regardless of the adult's raised voice or sobs?

REMEMBER...

Do not use any version of the word 'attachment' unless you are qualified to do so, which most of us are not. Do not use the word 'bond' either. Describe exactly what you see; paint a picture.

If there are pets in the home, how are they cared for? There are strong links between the abuse of animals and the abuse of women and children.

Unannounced visits

Sometimes it may be necessary to visit unannounced. But quite rightly, we have to justify why we are going to visit unannounced. This is usually because we think the family is not being honest with us about who is in the home, who is caring for the children, whether someone in the home is misusing substances, etc.

Case example: An unannounced visit

I was working with the mother of two young children. The father of the children was a convicted sex offender and he had been assessed as being at high risk of re-offending.

There were no concerns about the mother's care of the children, but we were concerned she was minimising the risk from their father, and wanted to be in a relationship with him.

The children were the subject of child protection plans, and the contingency plan was that if the mother got back together with the father, we would apply to remove the children from her care.

It got to the point where I just knew they were back together, but I could not prove it. I, along with different colleagues, did a number of unannounced home visits. Most professionals, including social workers, do not have the right to search a property, but during one visit the mother seemed particularly anxious and kept looking towards a closed door. I asked if anyone else was in the property and she said not. A short while later I heard coughing coming from behind the closed door. Sure enough, it was the father.

Unannounced visits play an essential role in the child protection process. In the second serious case review in the case of Peter Connolly, the review states, 'The value of an unannounced visit by the social worker was demonstrated in bringing the injuries to Peter to light.'[5]

5   Department for Education (2010) *Haringey Local Safeguarding Children Board. Serious Case Review. 'Child A.'* November 2008. Available at www.gov. uk/government/uploads/system/uploads/attachment_data/file/182527/first_ serious_case_review_overview_report_relating_to_peter_connelly_dated_ november_2008.pdf

REMEMBER...

Never make assumptions. Do not assume that because the room you have been shown into is immaculate, the rest of the house will be too. Do not assume that every child in the home is treated the same way. We should be permanently professionally curious, and our work must be evidence-based.

Everything in this chapter emphasises the importance of our observational skills, and using those to build the evidence we have, to see the world from the child's perspective. Just as a mother or father must prioritise their child, so must we, as professionals, be clear about and prioritise what matters most. Remember, it does not always matter if there are crumbs all over the floor and the washing up has not been done, but it does matter that the home is a safe, secure and nurturing place for every child.

6 Further Areas of Complexities for Professionals

There is a myth that children who are horrifically abused and neglected are hidden away, unknown to us all. This is untrue. Almost all are known to universal services, that is, health services and education services, if they are in education, and around half are known to social care. Each of the chapters so far has described the issues that we deal with all the time. This chapter considers further areas of complexities for professionals.

We should always remember that with all the other power imbalances and challenges I have written of throughout this book, children who come into the groups discussed further below will be even more vulnerable, because it is often these children who are overlooked, and we must therefore be aware of the increased sensitivities and additional vulnerabilities in our work and in our communication with them.

Working with children from the black and minority ethnic (BME) community

The last census in England and Wales, which admittedly was in 2011, said that 86 per cent of the population was White/British.[1] Although that figure will have changed since 2011, the majority of people who live in England and Wales are White/British, and

---

1   Office for National Statistics (2012) 'Ethnicity and National Identity in England and Wales 2011.' Available at www.ons.gov.uk/ons/dcp171776_290558.pdf

what that means is that the majority of the workforce will be White/British.

We have to guard against perpetrators of abuse hiding behind anything, including their race, religion, ethnicity or culture, but there may be values held and genuine causes for concern that a family has that we need to respect, and we must always be sensitive and respectful with every single family we work with. For example, if there is a male social worker and a referral has come in about a 15-year-old Muslim girl from a devout Muslim family, it may be completely unacceptable for the family for that male social worker to see the girl alone, or even that there is a male social worker at all. This is a view that should be respected and accepted.

It is not difficult to find out about practices in particular ethnic groups. There are so many different organisations you can find through the internet. I have often telephoned organisations and just explained that I am about to start working with a family from…and I need to know something about the culture before I go in and as I work with that family. In fact, just last week I had a very helpful conversation with a man at the Cameroonian High Commission. Many local authorities also have information pages about different faiths and cultures.

What we know is that if a family from the BME community *is* abusing their child, the first thing some families will do is accuse workers of being racist, which is extremely powerful, and may result in the case being closed without the evidence being assessed. No one wants to be accused of racism, with everything it means, so what do we White/British workers do? We turn a blind eye. We know this happens because children from the BME community are under-represented when we consider children who are subject to a child protection plan, but over-represented when we consider serious case reviews. What that tells us, in crude terms, is that we are not recognising the maltreatment of these children. What we have to do is strip away skin colour, race, religion, culture and ethnicity. All we need to ask is, 'Would I consider this to be maltreatment of a White/British child?', and if the answer to that is 'yes', then it is maltreatment.

A child is a child, and every child who lives in the country should be offered the same level of protection.

Working with alleged perpetrators from the black and minority ethnic community

There can be an increased sensitivity when an alleged perpetrator is from the BME community, and just as with a child we must strip everything away – other than that they are children, we must do the same with alleged perpetrators.

Case example: Beyond racism

What came out of the inquiry undertaken by Alexis Jay[2] into child sexual exploitation in Rotherham from 1997–2013 was that, historically, the police dared not act against Asian youths for fear of allegations of racism. As well as that, several staff described their nervousness about identifying the ethnic origins of perpetrators for fear of being thought racist; others remembered clear direction from their managers not to do so. The report goes on to say:

> Within the Council, we found no evidence of children's social care staff being influenced by concerns about the ethnic origins of suspected perpetrators when dealing with individual child protection cases, including child sexual exploitation. In the broader organisational context, however, there was a widespread perception that messages conveyed by some senior people in the Council and also the Police, were to 'downplay' the ethnic dimensions of child sexual exploitation.

The report concludes, 'People must be able to raise concerns without fear of being labelled racist.'

When we are working with a family from the BME community, too often we accept the family saying, 'It's cultural', without considering

---

2   Rotherham Metropolitan Borough Council (2014) Independent Inquiry into Child Sexual Exploitation in Rotherham (1997–2013). Available at www. rotherham.gov.uk/downloads/file/1407/independent_inquiry_cse_in_rotherham

the impact on the child. Just as with race, we need to be stripping culture away and asking the same question, 'Would I consider this abusive with another child?'

Again, what we see from serious case reviews is that we have accepted abusive practice because the family has said it is cultural and no one wants to offend.

Case example: Diamond Dwomah

Diamond was a ten-month-old baby girl who had lived with her family in the London Borough of Waltham Forest. When she died, the cause of death was declared to be 'pneumonia with further causations being the chronic aspiration of gastric content. There was aspiration of food material in the airways with a surrounding acute inflammation. Evidence of previous aspiration was also seen by the presence of multiple areas of acute inflammatory response. These were identified as food from recent and old feeds suggesting possible abuse by "force feeding".'[3]

What came from the serious case review was that the baby was being force fed, as an older sibling had been to the degree that they had had to have plastic surgery to repair the damage done by a feeding cup. The conclusion of the serious case review was that, 'Practitioners completing assessments need to sensitively consider the culture of a family. This includes understanding the reasons for parenting practices and the impact on the child.'

Case example: Children T and R

Child T was killed by his mother in February 2010, in the London Borough of Barking and Dagenham, at a time when both he and his sibling were the subject of child protection plans and about to become the subject of care proceedings.

Child T was 12 at the time of his death. He had severe learning difficulties, and was believed to have had a disorder on the autistic spectrum.

---

3   Waltham Forest Safeguarding Children Board (2011) *Serious Case Review. Child W.* Available at www.walthamforest.gov.uk/Documents/2011_10_21_ executive_summary_child_w_v4_-_final.pdf

Child T's parents were from families of Indian origin, and the family was Sikh.

The family had been known to social care for many years because of concerns of maltreatment of the children. The mother had withdrawn the children from school and said she was going to home educate them because of her unhappiness with the school. She wrote letters of complaint to all the agencies involved, making accusations of racism, lack of cultural sensitivity and unnecessary interference in family life.

What came from the serious case review[4] was that:

On a large number of occasions the mother gave professionals 'cultural' or 'religious' explanations as to why she did not want to use a service, why she was parenting the children in a particular way or to complain about services. At times she complained that services were being 'insensitive' or that white workers did not 'understand her culture' and then withdrew from the service or demanded to have the worker changed. These complaints and comments were not valid or justified, but professionals and agencies frequently failed to question or challenge these views. Overall professionals attributed too much weight to the mother's ethnicity and religion in explaining her behaviour, and insufficient attention to her individual psychology and personal history. They lacked confidence in dealing with a service user from a minority ethnic group.

REMEMBER...

The first question to ask is, 'Would I consider this to be maltreatment of a White/British child?', and if the answer to that is 'yes', then it is maltreatment.

Communication

Some children from minority ethnic groups will be completely assimilated within British culture (whatever that is), and there may

4   Barking and Dagenham Safeguarding Children Board (2015) Serious Case Review. Available at www.bardag-lscb.co.uk/Publications/Pages/SeriousCaseReview.aspx

be no cultural issues in how we communicate. For others, this will not be the case. And there will be some children for whom English is not their first language, who speak English very well, and other children who may speak little or no English, or who do, but they have to translate for their parents who speak no English. All these different circumstances will bring issues that you need to consider.

Just as with any family you are about to start working with, do your homework first, and if that family is from a minority ethnic group, you need to find out about the culture and whether there are particular ways you should, or should not, communicate.

Case example: Cultural differences

Many years ago I was working in a school in Nepal. Many of the children and the teachers boarded because they lived so far away. One weekend I had asked the girls who were boarding to tidy up their dormitory, which was a mess. They were lying on the floor, messing around and laughing. After a couple of attempts to get them moving, in my limited Nepali, I poked one of the girls on her bottom with my foot. There were audible gasps, and all of the girls looked horrified. I did not know what I had done, and they explained to me that in the Hindu religion feet are regarded as unclean because they touch the ground. When the girls explained, I was mortified at what I had done. They knew it was an innocent gesture and were very understanding, but it has stayed with me because I was embarrassed to have done something so offensive within their religion.

You will also need to think about whether the child you are working with knows what constitutes abuse, in this country. For example, within the child's culture it may be acceptable for her to be beaten if she is disobedient. Every child who lives in this country is entitled to be protected by the laws of this country, and so you may need to explain the difference to her. (This could be true of any child, thinking that what their parents do to them must be allowed, but could be additionally complicated.) Just be aware of cultural differences and, as always, do not make assumptions.

Communicating with children for whom English is not their first language

You will need to make a judgement about whether you use an interpreter or not. Again, do your homework and make sure you are prepared. It is a waste of everyone's time if you visit a family for the first time and they do not speak English. Sometimes this cannot be avoided, but in the majority of cases someone will know whether language is likely to be an issue. Speak to another professional you know who has already seen the family, and ask what the situation is.

With children, if you have to use an interpreter, they will not only have to speak to a stranger about very private matters, but on top of that, they will have someone from their own community who will then know their business. Particular care needs to be taken in an area when there are not many people from that minority ethnic group there, and if you use an interpreter, the child may not want to speak in front of them. Also, find out about whether there are gender issues with the interpreter, that is, a young girl and a male interpreter. All these things need to be considered. Just as when we are working with children with learning disabilities, however, we cannot be expected to know everything – so find someone who does.

Case example: Using the right interpreter

I was working with a young girl from Pakistan. Her English was very limited, and there were concerns of physical and sexual abuse, her father being the alleged perpetrator. I knew I would need an interpreter, but the difficulty was finding someone the girl would feel comfortable to speak in front of – as well as speaking to me, a stranger from a different culture.

First of all, I had to find out what language the family spoke – there are many languages in Pakistan. I found out they spoke Punjabi and I then had to find an interpreter – this was in an area where there was not a big Pakistani community. Luckily my manager agreed that we should bring someone in from outside, as the community was too small. I arranged for an interpreter to come from a nearby city, and made sure she was female. When I met with her I was talking about how difficult it can be in these circumstances.

She was extremely helpful, and said she would look into whether there may be anyone closer. A few days later she contacted me and told me about a teacher in a school in our area who spoke Punjabi. Because that teacher understood about confidentiality, because of the nature of her work, she became our interpreter. It was not ideal, but the best we could do because we were working closely with the family, and the local authority always has to balance best practice with cost.

Female genital mutilation

In the UK, female genital mutilation is a criminal offence. It is also illegal to arrange for a child to be taken abroad for female genital mutilation. It is estimated that 66,000 women in England and Wales have undergone female genital mutilation, and over 24,000 girls are estimated to be at risk.[5]

It is practiced in more than 29 countries across Africa, parts of the Middle East, South East Asia and countries where migrants from female genital mutilation-affected communities live.

Professionals who work in this field believe that the best way of stopping it is by empowering women and girls to say 'no' to female genital mutilation, and to enable them to act as leaders and advocates in their own communities.

The most usual way professionals know there is female genital mutilation within the family is when a woman is giving birth.

There is no specific age when it is done – it is performed on infants, girls and women of all ages. The age at which girls are cut can vary widely from country to country, and even within countries. Most often it happens before a girl reaches puberty.

There are several things that we, as practitioners, need to be mindful of:

---

5   Health Visiting and School Nursing Programmes: Supporting Implementation of the New Service Model. Leaflet No. 5: Domestic Violence and Abuse – Professional Guidance. Department of Health. Available at www.gov.uk/government/uploads/system/uploads/attachment_data/file/211018/9576-TSO-Health_Visiting_Domestic_Violence_A3_Posters_WEB.pdf

› With school-aged children, the most likely time for it to happen is at the start of the summer holidays because this will give the girls time to heal before they are seen by professionals again.

› Female genital mutilation is not a term that is used by those that communities/families that practice it. The most common term is 'cutting', but it is called different things in different communities, so again, do your research.

› It is not a religious practice.

› As with every other type of abuse, do not turn a blind eye. Do not make assumptions, but if you have any concerns it is likely to happen, do something about it.

Socioeconomic groups

For many reasons, the majority of families we work with in the child protection arena are in the lowest socioeconomic groups. This is not to say that only families in lower socioeconomic groups maltreat their children, but it is these families that face greater adversities in terms of poverty, housing, lower educational standards and poor health. Money brings power and power brings protection. We must never forget that just as with domestic abuse, child abuse crosses all socioeconomic groups, but it can be more effectively hidden in families with money and status. When we do hear about child abuse in a family of middle or high socioeconomic status, our reaction is often very different. There is often an assumption that that child cannot be being maltreated because the family lives in a big house and the child is dressed in designer clothes. Of course this is nonsense. You may not see as much physical neglect in children from higher socioeconomic groups, but emotional neglect may be just as prevalent, as may other types of maltreatment.

When such a family hears that social care has become involved, they may well threaten legal action, or bring their lawyer to the meetings, or complain to their local MP. If you have ever sat in a meeting where this has happened, you will know that professionals become frozen in fear that they will say something they should not. The focus on the child is completely lost, and it all becomes about the parents, just as we saw in the East Cheshire case mentioned earlier in Chapter 3. It is a highly effective tactic.

Case example: Abuse of middle class children

A referral came into our team when I was working in a duty team. The concern was from a teacher who used to go to the pub after school. Every time he went, he saw a pupil from the school who was nine years old. She was being 'babysat' by a man who would spend the evening getting increasingly drunk, and the child would be completely unsupervised. The teacher also described the pub as 'very dodgy'.

We looked into it and it turned out that the mother was a single parent and she was a politician. There was a big discussion in the office about who was going to ring her up because of her status. Eventually my team manager said, 'You can do it Joanna because you are posh and you won't be intimidated by her.' That sums this issue up. Some people, understandably, intimidate us, and this takes our focus away from the child.

I did telephone her and she could not have been more disgusted, or disdainful, that a social worker had deigned to telephone her and question her. She really did say, 'Do you know who I am?'

She refused to acknowledge there was any problem, and I am ashamed to say that we did just close the case. We did say to the teacher to tell us if it carried on. On reflection, I suspect if that mother had been from a lower socioeconomic group, we would not have left it at that.

Working with teenagers

Always remember that in the UK, a child is a child until they are 18.

Working with each age group presents its own challenges, but this group is perhaps the most challenging. We cannot 'do' to this age group as we 'do' to younger children. With younger children, the court makes a decision about their future, or the parents agree, and that is what happens – they go to the foster parents or to an aunt 50 miles away. With this age group, the young person needs to be part of the decision-making process, or they will just vote with their feet.

Case example: Involving teenagers in decisions

I was working with a 13-year-old, Tom, who lived with his father in a small city in a rural county. There had been ongoing concerns about Tom's life, and the fact that his father was taking no responsibility for Tom and not caring for him. There were also concerns that Tom's father was using Tom as a drugs runner. Tom had lived with chronic neglect for most of his life, and was desperate for love and stability. It reached the point where the professionals agreed that the risk to Tom was too great, and as well as that, Tom wanted to go into care. Tom's father put up a bit of a fight, but it was the professionals' view that this was only because he would be losing his runner and general skivvy. Tom's father agreed for Tom to go into care. There were no extended family members, so we agreed that I would find foster carers for Tom. The aim was to find a long-term placement, a family with whom he could live and have some stability.

Because of the limited number of foster carers available, the only placement was in a remote village, 15 miles from the city Tom lived in. As I drove Tom out of town, he pointed to a field and said, 'Is that a sheep?' Although he had lived in this rural county for 13 years, he had never left the city. When we arrived in the village I started to feel a sense of foreboding. How was this city child going to cope in a village, in the middle of nowhere, with no public transport? We were shown into the cottage by friendly, warm foster carers, who offered us tea. The cottage was very old and quaint and full of beautiful things. We had just left a home that had rubbish piled up in the front garden, a front room which only had a broken sofa, covered in piles of dirty clothes and dog hair, and a kitchen that was piled high with washing up and rubbish, with dog excrement on the floor. The foster mother brought in the tea, and on the tray were cups and saucers. Tom looked at me as if to say, 'What have you done to me?' I realised that this was not going to work. It was nothing to do with the foster carers. They were kind and considerate, but they were from another world, and Tom had been taken away from everything that he knew and that was familiar to him. I might as well have put him on Mars. He was completely isolated in this alien world, and within a few days he had run away, back to his father. He went back to what he knew, what was familiar to him.

It took a lot of work to persuade Tom that care would be a better alternative for him, and much greater thought about the right place for him to be. It was a real lesson to me that although we often do not have a great choice of placements, it is better to hold out for the right one, or you jeopardise your chances of that teenager leaving an abusive home.

Some people feel that it is 'too late' when they are working with this age group, older children, and particularly with teenagers. I have heard so many people say, 'I only like working with little children because you really can change their lives but not the older ones. It's too late for them; if they're off the rails there's nothing you can do. It's better to focus on the little ones.'

This view couldn't be more wrong. It used to be thought that brain development was set at an early age. While it is still accepted that a large percentage of brain development happens before a child is three, neuroscientists are increasingly understanding that the brain is in a constant state of neuroplasticity, which means it is changing all the time, and there is a second stage of major re-organisation in the brain, and that is during adolescence. There is much written about this now, including an article written by David Dobbs in the *National Geographic*, which sums up recent findings.[6] What this means is that there is always hope. The teenage brain is hugely adaptive, and therefore the 15-year-old who has lived with years of maltreatment is not beyond change. This is your chance to help affect positive change for that child, and how we work with these children is crucial. Things can get better for that child, and we can play a part in improving their lives, but what we must not do is tell them what is happening, or tell them what to do. We must work collaboratively with them, exploring what the options are and what that might mean.

6   Dobbs, D. (2011) 'Teenage brains.' *National Geographic*, October. Available at http://ngm.nationalgeographic.com/2011/10/teenage-brains/dobbs-text

Child sexual exploitation

It would be impossible to write a book about child protection and not mention child sexual exploitation, given the current climate. People who have considerable expertise have written much about it, but what I want to draw attention to here is the practical aspect of working with victims.

In the recent child sexual exploitation case in Oxford, Operation Bullfinch, which was the joint investigation launched by Thames Valley Police and Oxford County Council Social Services in May 2011, into suspected serious sexual offences against a number of children and young people, they made a conscious decision right at the beginning that they would not talk about potential victims as 'young people' or 'teenagers'; they would refer only to them as 'children'. The thinking behind this was that it would keep professionals focused on the fact that the victims, if they are under 18, are children. As soon as we use the term 'young people' it makes us think of autonomy, emancipation, young people making lifestyle choices, and calling them children reminded professionals that these were children who were being abused, not young people making lifestyle choices.

The previous section has talked of the complexities of working with teenagers, and everything written there also applies here. While not all victims of child sexual exploitation are teenagers, the majority are, although we are now seeing younger and younger children becoming victims. Whatever the child's age, remember that victims do not often see themselves as victims, and the perpetrator may be offering the child a life that seems to be much more exciting and more nurturing. This is one of the greatest challenges for professionals working in this field, and it is time, understanding, commitment, and honest, open working with the child that will give us the greatest chance of making a difference.

Although organisations such as Barnardo's have been working in this field for many years, for many, frontline professionals seem to be almost at the beginning of the process. What comes from serious case reviews is that professionals grapple with this type of abuse, partly because for too long it has not been recognised, but also because of what choices we have. Our services are not set up for working with this age group, or this complex area. We cannot lock all these children up, so how can we keep them safe when, very often, because of the grooming process and everything that has happened, they see themselves as having no choice but to remain with the perpetrators?

My advice would be to always seek expert help from those who work in the field all the time. Social workers and other frontline child protection workers cannot be expected to know everything about everything, so go to the workers who do, just as we should with domestic abuse, mental ill health, substance abuse, attachment disorders, and all the other complex areas of our work.

Children who have children who enter the child protection system

When a child becomes pregnant, sometimes we lose the focus on that child, and she is no longer seen as a child in her own right but as the mother of the unborn baby. As we have already established, teenagers are a particularly vulnerable group, and the girl who becomes pregnant becomes more vulnerable.

Case example: The invisibility of a pregnant teenager

A 15-year-old girl who was pregnant, was murdered by her father. What came from the serious case review was that although she was a vulnerable child, who was the subject of a child protection plan because of her abusive father, the moment she became pregnant she was only seen as the mother of the unborn baby. Her own needs became invisible. The unborn baby was made the subject of a child protection plan and her own case was closed because it was thought that her needs could be met through the plan for her unborn baby. She was still living in the abusive home, had an abusive partner herself, and had become more vulnerable because she was pregnant, but all of this was overlooked.

According to a recent report[7] published by the think tank The Centre for Social Justice, 22 per cent of female care leavers become teenage parents, which is three times the national average. According to the Centre: 'Young people from a care background are particularly vulnerable to early pregnancy because they can have an idealised view of what a "happy family" is. Their loneliness can mean they desire unconditional love from a baby, but they may not realise how demanding parenthood is.'

I have met many girls over the years who have grown up in abusive homes who believe that if they have a baby, everything will be alright because they will be given a home and their baby will love them. It is completely understandable that these children think that – everybody wants and everybody deserves a loving, stable home. The gap lies with our system and the lack of genuine support and nurturing there is for these young people. Evidence is clear that when the support is put in place, teenage pregnancies reduce, but that support is not universal.

REMEMBER...

A child is a child until they are 18, and regardless of whether the child becomes pregnant and then becomes a mother, we must never forget that the mother is still a vulnerable child herself.

Children with disabilities

Research on the protection of children with disabilities indicates that they are more at risk of being abused than non-disabled children.[8] However, they are less likely than other vulnerable children to become the subject of child protection plans. We also know that

---

7   The Centre for Social Justice (2015) *Finding their Feet: Equipping Care Leavers to Reach their Potential.* Available at www.centreforsocialjustice.org.uk/UserStorage/pdf/Pdf%20reports/Finding.pdf

8   Sullivan, P.M. and Knutson, J.F. (2000) 'Maltreatment and disabilities: a population-based epidemiological study.' *Child Abuse and Neglect* 24(10), 1257–1273.

just as with children from the BME community, children with disabilities are under-represented when we consider children who are subject to a child protection plan, but over-represented when we consider serious case reviews. Again, what this tells us is that we are not considering that these children are being maltreated before they die. Most children with disabilities will be known by a number of agencies, so they are not children who are hidden away, that no one knows about.

So why does it happen? Why is this group of children at greater risk, and why are we not seeing their maltreatment? Why are we not doing something about it?

Children with disabilities are at greater risk of maltreatment for many reasons. They may be more dependent on their parents and other carers. There may be a number of people involved in their intimate care. They may not be able to tell anyone what is happening. They may not know what is happening is wrong and have less to judge it against because they may be more isolated. Having a child with a disability puts a huge strain on the family – there are more likely to be relationship breakdowns between the parents, so there are more single-parent families. And there are more families living in poverty when there is a child with a disability. In many areas there is not a lot of support for the family – the benefit system can be a minefield, and they may not have the energy to work their way through it when they are only getting two hours sleep at a time. The greater the pressure any parents are under, the greater the risk to the child, and having a child with a disability adds considerable pressure. If the child has a learning disability, will they be believed if they tell anyone they are being abused, particularly if that child is always telling stories that are patently untrue? The information gets lost, and the receiver of the information may think it is just another story. It is also very rare for a case to get to court if the alleged victim is a child with a learning disability, and perpetrators know that.

Why do we, as professionals, find it so hard to recognise maltreatment of a child with a disability? Very often professionals feel desperately sorry for the parent, who may be struggling against all the adversities, but the trouble is that this may cloud our judgement

– we do not see the maltreatment, or we have a different threshold for neglect. It can be easy to put the injuries down to the disability, but what we have to remember, as I have repeated often in this chapter, is that we must not have different thresholds for different children or different groups of children. If you would consider it maltreatment of one child, then it is maltreatment of all.

7 Working More Effectively with Families

In each chapter so far, we have considered how we can work effectively with families, and how we can improve how we work. The aim of this final chapter is to cover everything that has not been covered before, and to give some more general ideas.

Language

How often do you go to a meeting, and as you go round the table doing introductions, someone says 'I'm Sarah. I'm an SDC from FLT', and you carry on going round? I promise you, you will not be the only one who does not know what an 'SDC from FLT' means (remember Tudor Rose from the Introduction). If you, as a professional, are feeling inadequate because you do not know what that means and you think you should, imagine how much more intimidating this would be for the family members who are there. Everyone, most of all the family, needs to know who everyone is, who they work for, and what their role is.

Sometimes we professionals use jargon just because it is easier to do so, rather than explain what we actually mean, as highlighted by the example of 'appropriate' and 'inappropriate' in Chapter 1. Sometimes professionals use jargon because it makes them feel important and knowledgeable that they can use these terms and they know what they mean. But this is incredibly unhelpful. Throughout this book we have talked about the power imbalance between families and professionals, and if we go into a meeting with a family and use language like, 'We are going to have to do a Section 47', or 'We want to go for ICOs', imagine how that would feel for the family this is being said to.

Over the years I have heard professionals talk like this a million times. Each time I wince, and then try to explain to the family what it is they actually mean. And there is one particular example that sticks in my mind.

Case example: Avoiding jargon

I had just qualified as a social worker and had joined a local authority child protection team. I was sent out on a visit to watch and learn from an experienced social worker.

The case was a single mother who had four children. The concerns were that the children were being neglected, and there was very little supervision of these four young children because the mother was a heavy drinker; at times the children were completely unsupervised, because the mother had left them alone while she went to the pub, or she had gone out to acquire alcohol, or because she would just pass out.

On this occasion a neighbour had rung the police because the four-year-old was out in the street, the front door was open, and when the neighbour had called the mother, there did not seem to be anyone there.

When we arrived at the home, we found the mother semi-conscious, lying on the sofa with an almost empty bottle in her hand. She was so drunk she could hardly speak.

The experienced social worker lent over her and said, 'If you don't stop this drinking we are going to have to initiate CP procedures.' The mother lay, cross-eyed, mouth slack.

It was utterly pointless trying to have a reasonable conversation with the mother at that time anyway, but to use such ridiculous language just compounded the error. The most important thing was to ensure the safety of the children, which did happen, and then to speak to the mother, when she was sober, and have that conversation with her then, without using any jargon.

The terminology we use is crucial because it sets out what we are dealing with, but make sure that it is correct. I often hear terms banded about: 'She's an alcoholic', 'He's definitely got a personality disorder' etc. etc. In each of these cases, what is the evidence? Has there been a clinical diagnosis of alcoholism, or is it that every time you see the mother she is swaying, smells strongly of alcohol and you often see bottles strewn across her living room floor? If it is the latter, this is useful information, but say exactly that – do not say someone is an alcoholic unless you know there has been a clinical diagnosis.

The term 'personality disorder' is used freely and often inaccurately. Again, only use it if you know there has been a clinical diagnosis, but always describe the behaviour that you see.

I have written about attachment theory in Chapter 1 on neglect. This is probably the term I see written the most freely: 'She had a good attachment', or 'There was an insecure attachment', or 'There was a good bond between the mother and the baby.' Peter Connelly was described as having a good attachment with his mother[1] during one of the professional's home visits, as well as a good bond. I would say that most of us, definitely including me, are not qualified to make such a statement. It is a very broad term that will mean different things to different people. Unless you are a psychologist with expertise in this field, rather than use the term 'attachment' or 'bond', say what you are actually seeing.

When we use these words with the mother, will she understand? 'We are concerned about your bond with Lucy.' 'We are worried about Peter's attachment to you.' Spell it out, say something like, 'We are worried because when we see you with Lucy you often ignore her, you do not pick her up unless she is crying, and when you do pick her up you always seem to hold her away from you, and you don't seem to be making eye contact with her, or talk to her', and then explain why these things matter.

---

1   Department for Education (2010) *Haringey Local Safeguarding Children Board. Serious Case Review. 'Child A.'* November 2008. Available at www.gov. uk/government/uploads/system/uploads/attachment_data/file/182527/first_ serious_case_review_overview_report_relating_to_peter_connelly_dated_ november_2008.pdf

It is easy to use all these terms, but it is unprofessional, and we do the families we work with an injustice. A label sticks and then assumptions are made, and sometimes it can take many years to reverse something that has become set in stone because one person wrote it erroneously in a report.

Case example: Avoiding vague terms

The term 'person posing a risk to children' replaced the term 'Schedule 1 offender' in light of the Home Office Guidance ('Guidance on Offences Against Children', Home Office Circular 16/2005). A 'person posing a risk to children' indicates that the person has been identified as presenting a risk, or potential risk, to children, not only as a result of the nature of his or her offence, but also as a result of a further assessment to determine if s/he should be regarded as presenting a continued risk of harm to children. Home Office Circular 16/2005 contains a list of offences that should operate as a trigger to such further assessment.

I undertook a serious case review where two of the adults in the extended family were known to pose a risk to children. As part of the review we held conversations with the frontline professionals who were working with the family at the time of the incident. Several of these professionals used this term to describe one, or both, of these adults. When we asked what had actually happened, not one single person could tell us. How could they possibly have assessed the level of risk to the children in the home when some of the professionals did not know either adult was considered to pose a risk to the children? Some knew one was, but none knew what the offence actually was. Some had a vague idea, but none knew for sure.

'Posing a risk to children' is an amorphous term that tells us nothing about what offence the perpetrator has committed, or how many offences have been committed, or how great the risk of re-offending is. If you are working with a family and the term 'posing a risk to children' is used about about anyone who is having contact with a child, find out what the offence was and the likelihood of re-offending. In child protection cases the social worker should get this information from the police and the probation service, and share the information with the other professionals involved.

REMEMBER...

Regarding 'person posing a risk to children', the social worker should always find out what the offence was and the likelihood of re-offending from the police and probation, and share this information with the other professionals working with the family.

The same would apply to any other label that has been put on the person. In a multi-agency group working around a child, the social worker will always be the lead professional in child protection cases, but it is the responsibility of the entire group to ensure they are dealing with factually correct information. Be the one to question a term that is used if you think it might not be correct.

REMEMBER...

Never use jargon and never use acronyms when working with families.

Explain

Always explain what is happening and what is likely to happen. Make it very clear why you are involved and what the concerns are. This is where banning the use of the words 'appropriate' and 'inappropriate' comes into its own again. We say to a parent that we are worried about John's 'inappropriate language with his peers', but this means nothing. To the parent it might be absolutely fine to tell everyone to 'F*** off', so by using the word 'inappropriate', you have told the parent nothing. Explain what the language being used is, and why it is not okay to use it at school, or anywhere else.

If you ask many families what having a child protection plan means, they will say that it means social services are going to take the child away. Families are given literature explaining what the process is beforehand, but nothing substitutes for an explanation of what the process is.

When I reflect back on my practice I often wince at what I used/used not to do. How much time did I actually spend explaining to families what the child protection process is? The honest answer to that would be not nearly enough. What we should be doing is explaining what being the subject of a child protection plans means, and that if we were that worried we would be going to court because we wanted to take that child into care, but we are not doing that because we believe and we hope that with the right amount of support, the parent or carer will be able to make the changes that need to happen in order for the child to be safe and to thrive. This is what we should be emphasising, that there is hope. It is not saying that we think the parent/carer cannot do it, but that we think they can, if we give them the right support.

So often when I meet with families, when I am doing a serious case review, the mother will say to me, 'I didn't know what they wanted', and she wasn't aware who half the people working with the family were. This will not always be for lack of trying on the professional's part, but sometimes we speak in our own language that is not understood, assuming that the mother will understand everything. We use so many words that are unintelligible. If you have a child on a child protection plan, try writing down the areas where change is needed, in clear, constructive, simple words, and give it to the mother and suggest she puts it somewhere she can always see it, so there can be no doubt about your expectations. Write a list of all the professionals' names, with a few words about who they work for and what they do, to help the family understand who everyone is.

What I have said about child protection conferences is true of any work that we do with families. Always explain and keep it simple – do not hide behind jargon and acronyms. As I said in the Introduction, the starting point for all of us working in child protection should be that the best place for a child to grow up in is within their own home, and our best chance of achieving that is if we are honest and open with the families we work with, and this includes being clear, in our language and in our intentions.

Empathy

The clearest definition of empathy that I have come across is that it is the ability to put oneself in someone else's shoes, to see the world from their perspective.

It is really important that in all our work we are empathic. Never forget that the majority of parents we are working with in the child protection arena will have come from an abusive home themselves, or that the maltreatment is happening because of the parent's own unmet mental health needs, or substance misuse, which is a known coping mechanism for personal trauma.

We often talk about women as victims, and even female perpetrators of abuse or violence as being victims themselves, because many of them are, but the same is also true of men. Our prisons are full of men who have been abused as children. In a Ministry of Justice report, *Prisoners' Childhood and Family Backgrounds*,[2] 24 per cent of the prisoners stated that they had been in care at some point during their childhood. Those who had been in care were younger when they were first arrested, and were more likely to be reconvicted in the year after release from custody than those who had never been in care. Twenty-nine per cent of the prisoners had experienced abuse, and 41 per cent had observed violence in the home as a child. Those who reported experiencing abuse or observing violence as a child were more likely to be reconvicted in the year after release than those who did not. Eighteen per cent of prisoners stated that they had a family member with an alcohol problem, and 14 per cent with a drug problem. Fifty-nine per cent of the prisoners stated that they had regularly played truant from school, 63 per cent had been suspended or temporarily excluded, and 42 per cent stated that they had been permanently excluded or expelled. Prisoners with these issues were more likely to be reconvicted on release than

---

2   Williams, K., Papadopoulou, V. and Booth, N. (2012) *Prisoners' Childhood and Family Backgrounds: Results from the Surveying Prisoner Crime Reduction (SPCR) Longitudinal Cohort Study of Prisoners.* Ministry of Justice Research Series 4/12. Available at www.gov.uk/government/uploads/system/uploads/attachment_data/file/278837/prisoners-childhood-family-backgrounds.pdf

those without. Of the contributors to the survey who fed into this research, 91 per cent were male.

So, while it may be true to say many female perpetrators of maltreatment have been victims of other types of abuse, at the hands of men, the same is also true of the fathers we work with.

As professionals, we are there to make judgements about children's safety and their welfare; we are not there to make personal judgements about their parents and carers, and as always, our best way of effecting change is to understand why parents behave the way they do.

Case example: Being empathic

The best practitioners show empathy towards families all the time. The best example I have heard of, although I have heard so many, was at a nursery school. It was in an affluent area, but there was one family that the school knew were really struggling financially.

There was a craze for coloured pencils, and the nursery was worried that the mother would feel she had to buy them, so they arranged a raffle, and fortunately, this little boy won the prize.

Be realistic

It is increasingly recognised that with neglect cases in particular, the most effective way to work with families is as small a number of professionals as possible working closely together, and yet the reality is very often that our services are not set up like that.

Case example: Professional overload

I was involved in a serious case review where a child had died. The family had been known to social care and other agencies for many years. The concerns were neglect and emotional abuse.

The mother, Hannah, was a single parent; she had three children under the age of six, one of whom had a physical and learning disability, and another a learning difficulty. The children had all been on and off child protection plans over the years, and it was one of the typical cases set out in Chapter 1 earlier, about neglect – when do we say enough is enough when things typically get worse, then better again? Tragically, in this case, one of the children died.

One of the things that came out of the serious case review was that for extensive periods of time Hannah had had nine different professionals working with her, all offering her some level of parenting advice.

Hannah was a mother who struggled with everything, including managing her finances and having the children in any kind of routine. Life was very chaotic.

The professional response to this, following procedures set out in the statutory guidance, was to put a child protection plan in place. The plan consisted of the expectation that Hannah would attend a range of specialist health appointments, both in the hospital and at home, for two of her children, attend meetings at the school because of her children's special needs, meet with the social worker every week, attend a children's centre with her youngest child, including drop-ins and groups, meet regularly with a family support worker from social care, meet with the health visitor regularly at home and in clinic, and meet with an early years worker from the children's centre. All this was put in place for a woman who struggled to put the tea on the table.

So when you are devising your child protection plan, or your child in need plan, or any other plan, be realistic. I have read so many child protection plans that are just a list of services we expect the mother to engage with, and it is entirely unrealistic that she will ever be able to achieve what we expect of her because our expectations are unrealistic. The expression 'setting her up to fail' comes to mind.

Sometimes you have to focus on what really needs to change today. You can have immediate, short-term and long-term aims, but do not overwhelm parents because you will not be helping them, and so you will not be helping the child.

I have read two serious case reviews recently where the professionals involved in the child protection plan knew that an immediate change was necessary. One of the cases involved chronic neglect and the youngest child had severe nappy rash. It was not getting any better, and the professionals met and spoke about it, along with the other concerns, and there were many, but for the three weeks of talking, that child still had nappy rash. It was so severe that when he was admitted to hospital, the paediatrician who examined him said he had never seen such a severe nappy rash. The other case was a child who needed medication because of chronic constipation. For two weeks the mother did not collect the prescription, and for that four weeks the constipation became worse and worse. If constipation is not relieved, the acid from the gut expels itself around the constipation, which again causes severe nappy rash. During this time all the professionals were telling the mother that she must collect the prescription, but she never did; in the end, one of the professionals did. What we have to remember is that children continue to suffer while we try to support and encourage the parent to take responsibility, but some things need to be sorted straight away.

Being realistic refers to what we expect of parents, but it also refers to what we offer children. Resources are scarce, but as the frontline worker working with the family, you must also advocate for the child. You have a responsibility to the child to make sure that whatever the service that is offered, it is the best it can be.

Case example: In the children's best interests

I had to place two siblings in an emergency. They were six and four, and were White/British children who had grown up in a predominantly white community, living with their parents.

Initially, when I made the request, I was told it was unlikely they could be placed together, but I insisted that they must be. (A report has recently come out by the Family Rights Group saying that 49 per cent of sibling groups in local authority care had been split up.[3]) Sometimes siblings are separated for legitimate reasons, but sometimes it is a practical issue.

As we came towards the end of the day and I was becoming increasingly concerned about a placement, the team called me and said they had a couple who would take the children together. I was

---

3   Ashley, C. and Roth, D. (2015) *What Happens to Siblings in the Care System?* Family Rights Group. Available at www.frg.org.uk/images/PDFS/siblings-in-care-final-report-january-2015.pdf

so pleased, but then they told me about the couple. They were a devout Muslim couple and they lived in a part of a city where 95 per cent of the population was of Asian origin. I was told that the mother would not be able to deal with us; everything had to be done through the father. The mother wore a full burka, including covering her face, when she left the home, or people came to the home, who she did not know.

I said the children could not go there. Everyone got very anxious and thought I was being racist/politically incorrect/offensive/ insensitive, and various other things. My view was absolutely nothing to do with the religion or the culture of the family; it was because for these two children, who were being taken from their mother, with whom they had always lived, it was going to be traumatic enough without placing them with a family from a completely different culture. I also thought that unless you are used to it, it may be frightening for a young child to see the woman who is caring for you put on a long black covering, including her face. Many children are terrified when they see Father Christmas close up, for example, and it may have had the same effect, and I did not think that was a risk worth taking for these children.

Eventually everyone calmed down and realised that this would not have been in the children's best interests, and another more suitable placement was found. It clearly demonstrated what we considered in the previous chapter, how anxious everyone becomes when we have to consider race/culture/religion or ethnicity.

Superficial working

No one has enough time; everyone has too many cases. Sadly this is the situation for most professionals. Of course this doesn't mean that there is not brilliant work being done, because there is, and there always will be, but in the world of child protection, we have fallen into a trap. We rush from one meeting to another, ticking boxes saying we have held this meeting within the required timescale, we have seen the child when we should have, but what we have to ask ourselves is, is what we are doing meaningful, or are we just rushing from one meeting to another, skimming the surface? This is what I see from serious case reviews. It is never a lack of commitment; it is just that no one has any time to really get to the heart of what is really going on in a particular family. The trouble is, if we only skim the surface, we can carry on like that for months and months with nothing really changing, whereas if we put the time in to really understand the family, our work will be much more effective, and therefore we will not need to work with that family for so long. Either we can put the right support in and the family can continue to care for that child, or we recognise it is not going to happen and look to seek alternative, permanent care for the child.

I wrote an article for *The Guardian* last year entitled 'Partnership agreements fail to keep children safe.'[4] I would go further than that. Partnership or written agreements are not worth the paper they are written on. Social workers put great stock on them, and they are used a lot. The trouble is that they are very often used with women who are victims of domestic abuse, and the agreement they sign says they will not let the father of the children have contact with them. I have done two serious case reviews recently, and in both cases the father had just been found guilty of the murder of one of his children; both men were perpetrators of domestic abuse. In both cases there was a written agreement in place. Social care had told the women that they could only keep the children in their care if they signed the written agreement. Both of these women, from different parts of the country, said to me, 'Of course I was going to sign it; otherwise they would have taken my children away.' They also told me that they did not know who to be more frightened of – the social worker, because of their power, or the ex-partner. Both women told me that as soon as the social worker left, the ex-partner was back in the door. These women could no more have stopped their partners coming back than they could have flown to the moon. How can a victim of domestic abuse possibly control her partner, or ex-partner, to the extent that he does what she tells him? Of course she cannot.

So always think very carefully about using partnership agreements. They might make us professionals feel reassured, and they might be useful as evidence when they are not adhered to, but

---

4   Nicolas, J. (2014) 'Partnership agreements fail to keep children safe.' *The Guardian*, 10 April. Available at www.theguardian.com/social-care-network/2014/apr/10/partnership-agreements-fail-keep-children-safe

they will do nothing to keep the child safer, and may, indeed, put both the mother and the children at greater risk.

In Chapter 3 we considered disguised compliance, and looked at a parent's capacity to change; this is relevant here too. We need to look at the house being tidy once, Johnie getting to school on time once, in the context of the last year, and not focus too much on the one good event, but look at it in the round.

How often have you written in a report that it is a strength that the family is attending appointments, it is a strength that they are engaging, and it is a concern if they are not? First of all, attending is not the same as engaging. When I was an employee, sometimes I had to go to meetings I did not want to go to. I attended, but I have to admit that I did not necessarily engage. There are some families that know professionals put great stock on them attending appointments, and so they go to everything, but this does not mean that they are engaging.

As always, everything must come back to the evidence. The evidence that someone is engaging will be that they are changing what they are doing and things are improving for the child.

If a family does not attend an appointment, we need to go deeper than just saying that it is concerning. If they miss a medical appointment for their child, it might be extremely concerning, but if they miss a meeting with a family support worker from social care, but they did meet the community family worker three days before, it might not be quite so serious. It may be a situation where we ask ourselves, 'Are we being realistic in the number of professionals we are expecting this parent to meet with?'

In Chapters 1 and 3 I have already written about the power of using multi-agency chronologies, as well as single-agency chronologies. I raise them again here to remind you of their usefulness.

Remember, too, what was written in Chapter 3 about a parent's capacity to change. Always think about the parent's motivation, as well as their mental capacity.

Communicating and sharing information between professionals

This is an issue that comes up in almost every serious case review that has ever been done. There is no doubt that we can work more effectively in this area too, even within the tight time constraints and heavy workloads we all have.

One of the first actions that takes place when a decision is made that there needs to be a serious case review is that a multi-agency chronology is put together. Each of the agencies that has been working with the family are asked to compile a chronology, and this is then amalgamated. As an author of serious case reviews, I read that chronology and very often, admittedly with the benefit of hindsight, wonder why that child was still in the home, with all these concerns. In every single serious case review I have done, and in many more beyond, what has come to light after the child has died, or suffered serious injuries, was that no one professional has had all the information. The question is, how can you effectively assess risk if you do not have all the information?

It is fundamental that in this hugely complex and challenging work, the frontline professionals who are working with a family on a daily or weekly basis know everything that everyone else does. Of course we cannot know what we do not know, but there are too many cases where different professionals have different pieces of the puzzle. As I have said before, much of our learning comes from serious case reviews, and we see this lack of information-sharing in them. Maybe the same issue doesn't arise in cases that do not end in tragedy, and that may be part of the reason why. We will never get to the point where we can prevent every child dying, but there is no doubt that we could do a better job than we do now if we became better at sharing what we know.

Challenge/healthy challenge/enquire

We are constantly told that we should challenge other professionals, that healthy challenge is good, but at the heart of this, if you challenge someone, what you are actually doing is saying that you think they are wrong, and this is what many people have a problem with, which is why they find it so hard.

It was a GP who suggested in a serious case review I was doing that we should use the word 'enquire' because it is less aggressive. I thought it was one of those things that is brilliant because it is so simple. The difference between someone saying 'Sorry, can I just stop you there. I don't actually think that's right because XYZ', and 'Sorry, can I just stop you there and ask you more about that because I am not sure I understand it' is vast, and you are likely to get a very different response. Whatever we may say, most of us do not like being challenged, but most of us are happy to explain further.

REMEMBER...

Enquiring is more constructive than challenging.

What does good working together look like?

Before you read on, ask yourself this question, and see what you come up with. I do this as an exercise with every group I work with, and invariably professionals come up with the following:

> sharing information

> communication

> keeping the child at the centre

> healthy challenge

> meetings well attended.

What I very rarely hear is anyone saying is, 'Things getting better for the child.' This is what good working together is. All of the points above are, of course, essential, but the nub of it all is that things get better for the child. Sometimes when I do a case review the frontline professionals will tell us how well they all worked together as a group of professionals, and then they describe what is set out here, the meetings were well attended, they all felt they could challenge each other, information was shared between professionals, etc., etc. The trouble is, what I am seeing is children who have been on a child protection plan for a year, then off for a year, then back on, and then finally taken into care. How can that be good working together, from the child's perspective? Processes may have been followed effectively, but it has taken three years in a child's short life to actually achieve a positive outcome that is sustainable, as opposed to 'Last week wasn't great but it is looking better this week.' When you think about how the brain develops, three years is a very long time.

Most local authorities and their partner agencies are introducing some form of multi-agency safeguarding hubs at point of entry to social care. They have been shown to be an effective way of sharing information between professionals at the initial stage, when the referral is made. What we need is for that information sharing to continue throughout.

In Scotland, practice guidance sets out the advantage of multi-agency chronologies,[5] and they are used more routinely. In some parts of England they are now being used in child protection cases, but they are not yet routine.

A good multi-agency chronology will keep you up to date with what is happening with a child. They also demonstrate clear patterns of behaviour or incidents.

Case example: The power of multi-agency chronologies

Until his death at the age of three, Bob had lived with his mother and father. The family had been known to social care since his birth because of concerns about both his parents misusing substances. Both were able to stop using illegal street drugs, and were on a methadone programme. Bob was the subject of a child protection plan for most of his life, as was his younger sister when she was born.

---

5   Donnelley, R.R. (2010) *Chronologies*. Practice Guide. Social Work Inspection Agency. Available at www.scotland.gov.uk/Resource/Doc/299703/0093436.pdf

One of the concerns the professionals working with the children had was the parents' lifestyle. They had no routine in place for the children, and life was very chaotic. The mother was on a high level of methadone and would often fall asleep in the many meetings she had around the children, when she managed to attend them. She missed many appointments, as did the father. So there was a general picture of chaos, no routine and missed appointments.

What came out of the serious case review was that neither parent missed a single appointment with either their prescribing psychiatrist or their drugs worker, with whom they had to meet every week or they would not get their prescription. Both parents had a very clear routine around their drug taking – they would take it in turns every day, so one remained with the children, and the mother never fell asleep in meetings with the psychiatrist or the drugs worker.

This information stood out very clearly when we received the multi-agency chronology, but for the frontline professionals working with the family, they were too close and were unable to see this.

What multi-agency chronologies can also do is highlight how unrealistic our expectations of families can be. They can also help to show families patterns that we are worried about.

'Them and us'

I have worked in social care for nearly 20 years, and there has always been a 'them and us'. When I was a residential social worker, the 'them' was the local authority social workers. When I worked in the voluntary sector, it was the statutory sector. When I was a local authority social worker, it was almost everybody else as well as senior managers who kept giving us new things to do because they didn't have anything better to do, and they had to do something to justify their enormous salaries, and now it is governments, civil servants and Ofsted! Whoever the 'them' is, it always feels as if it is 'us' doing all the work.

Myth: 'We are the only ones doing the work'

A few years ago I delivered a rolling programme of child protection training for frontline police officers. This meant that every two weeks, for six months, I would spend a day with 30–40 police officers.

Every session, without fail, the subject of social care's out-of-hours team would come up. The police would say, 'It's a group of social workers sitting around, drinking herbal tea and knitting while we do their work for them.' (That was the most polite version of what they think we social workers do en masse. Some others are unrepeatable here.) For these frontline officers, they get called to a domestic incident at 3am. The man is arrested, the mother has to go to hospital and there is a baby. The police either cannot get the information, or they establish that there is nowhere for the baby to go, so they ring social care's out-of-hours team and what happens…they get the answering machine. That officer has to deal with the arrest and all the paperwork around the incident, and they are left holding the baby, literally, because they cannot get hold of the social worker; meanwhile, their radio is going, calling them to the next incident, and the next and the next.

Every session I would ask how many social workers they thought were in the out-of-hours team, and they would say anywhere between four and ten, because it is a 'team'. The word 'team' conjures up lots of people, a group. Every session I would have to explain that in that area, the out-of-hours team consisted of three workers until midnight, and then it was two. They covered the whole geographical area of the city, and it was a large city, and they also covered cradle-to-grave services, meaning that they were also called to incidents with adults.

Once the police understood that, it did not give them the support that they really should have, but at least they understood that it was not a group of social workers sitting around doing nothing while they did all the work.

For the last seven years I have worked independently. I work with professionals from all agencies and at all levels, from director of children's services and chief executives to frontline workers. I work with statutory organisations, private organisations and voluntary organisations.

I work with the Department for Education and have worked with Ofsted, and what I see at every level, in every organisation, are professionals doing their absolute best to make children's lives better. In seven years of doing serious case reviews across the country, I have yet to see any individual practice that has really shocked me – naivety sometimes, perhaps a lack of knowledge, but rarely a cavalier attitude to the protection of children. Of course it does happen sometimes, but it is absolutely not the norm. What is much more likely is people working at weekends, working ridiculous hours, and the most extreme, a teacher who timed her pregnancy around a particular year group's GCSEs because she had some very vulnerable children in that year group.

There is no 'them and us'. One of the greatest life skills anyone in any job can have is empathy. This is what we need to do in this job because there will always be an explanation for why someone has not done what they were supposed to do, and rather than build up barriers between teams and between agencies, if we are going to do the best job we can to protect our most vulnerable children and improve their lives, we need to knock down those barriers and work together.

We must all work together, honestly and openly, and do the same with the families we work with. We must understand and support the family, where that is the right thing to do for the child, but in all of the work we do, we must never lose our focus on the child. This is why we do the work we do. These children are the parents of the future, and we can make a difference to their lives.

Index